LOVE

&

Verses

KENNETH E. SULLIVAN JR.

ISBN: 978-1-7341479-2-6 (Paperback)
978-1-7341479-3-3 (E-Book)

Library of Congress Control Number: 2019919222

Front cover image by Dream Church Graphics.
Book design by Prize Publishing House, LLC.

Printed by Prize Publishing House, LLC, in the United States of America.

First printing edition 2020.

Prize Publishing House
P.O. Box 9856
Chesapeake, VA 23321

www.PrizePublishingHouse.com

Contents

LOVE & VERSES I
A MATCH MADE IN HEAVEN

LOVE & VERSES II
WHAT A GIRL WANTS, WHAT A GUY NEEDS

LOVE & VERSES III
TEACH ME HOW TO LOVE

LOVE & VERSES IV
FIRE & DESIRE

LOVE & VERSES V
THE POWER COUPLE

LOVE & VERSES VI
REKINDLE THE FIRE

About the Author

Kenneth Sullivan, Jr. is a native of Indianapolis, Indiana. He has a Bachelor's degree from the College of Biblical Studies, formerly Crossroads Bible College, and a Masters of Christian Leadership from Indiana (Wesleyan Seminary). He is the Pastor of New Direction Church in Indianapolis, Indiana. He and his lovely wife Roxie Sullivan will celebrate 20 years of marriage in June 2020. They have three beautiful children: Gabrielle, Kennedy, and David.

Preface

Pastor Kenneth Sullivan, Jr. has had the privilege of seeing his parents married for nearly 50 years. He has also had the privilege of seeing both sets of grandparents enjoy healthy long satisfying marriages. God has also allowed him to have a strong and enjoyable marriage relationship as well. Pastor Sullivan wants to share some of the timeless principles he has learned from what he has observed in the marriage relationships of his parents and grandparents and from his own successful marriage relationship.

For the past 13 years he has had the privilege of performing over 40 weddings. He has also counseled numerous couples who have gone on to be married or who have contemplated marriage.

In 2015, Pastor Sullivan's church hosted a Christian reality dating show called *It Takes a Church*. The show was hosted by Natalie Grant and it was a wonderful experience for the church. It is still available to watch on Hulu and other platforms.

For the past five years of ministry Pastor Sullivan has taught a relationship series in the month of February at New Direction Church. These series have grown to be a blessing to countless marriages and couples.

There were times he wanted to quit, but he realized a relationship is like a flight, you may face turbulence, clouds may come and bad weather, but it smooths out.

Acknowledgements and Dedication

My Wife Roxie: I want to acknowledge and thank my wife and the love of my life, Roxie Sullivan. I want to thank you for being such a caring and considerate person and for loving me and supporting me in all my endeavors. You have been the greatest blessing in my life.

Parents: I want to thank my parents, who have been married for nearly 50 years, for modeling for my sisters and I what a true godly relationship looks like.

Grandparents: I want to acknowledge my grandparents on both sides of my family for helping to provide an example of true love and commitment.

Foreword

I am so excited that you get a chance to discover one of our nation's most powerful voices. Many themes run through the songs of our lives, and sometimes we need to see the words of the songs to really feel the impact. Pastor Sullivan does a great job at getting us back to the reality and the simplicity of love and romance. He shows us not only how to love, but also how to treasure our relationships. It is refreshing how he writes using some of our favorite songs. The nuggets dropped in this book are amazing and, if applied, will transform your love life.

- Dr. Marquis D. Boone

LOVE & VERSES I

A Match Made in Heaven

Genesis 2:20-24 (NKJV)

²⁰ So Adam gave names to all cattle, to the birds of the air, and to every beast of the field. But for Adam there was not found a helper comparable to him.

²¹ And the LORD God caused a deep sleep to fall on Adam, and he slept; and He took one of his ribs and closed up the flesh in its place. ²² Then the rib which the LORD God had taken from man He made into a woman, and He brought her to the man.

²³ And Adam said:

"This is now bone of my bones
And flesh of my flesh;
She shall be called Woman,
Because she was taken out of Man."

²⁴ Therefore a man shall leave his father and mother and be joined to his wife, and they shall become one flesh.

*E*veryone longs to find that special someone we might call a soulmate. The one whom it seems has been divinely sent and specifically designed to suit their needs. The perfect match. As Keshia Cole said a love "Sent from Heaven". There are literally millions of sites, services and even shows that advertise. With a call or click of the mouse, you can find the perfect person or match for you. Just to name a few (Millionaire Matchmaker, Christianmingle. com, and eHarmony). I do not think some of those avenues are all bad. In fact, I have had the privilege of marrying several couples who have met online. I do believe that if you are looking for a soulmate or a match made in Heaven you need to look to the maker of Heaven and Earth.

What we find here in Genesis 2:18-24 is literally a match made in Heaven. We are privy to share and to witness the very first wedding and marriage between a man and a woman. We see somewhat of a blueprint as we see the first marriage and we see the way God originally intended for it to work.

Marriage is not something that simply evolved over time. It is not something that man created out of convenience. Marriage is not something man made; it is something God made. We discover that in fact marriage and the home is the first institution God established. Before God established the government, school, and even the church, God established marriage. There are some things that we can learn from this first marriage that was truly a match made in Heaven.

**Adam and Eve were literally soulmates. They connected with each other based upon what was on the inside of them. They had an inward connection. That is important to note because a soulmate is not all about the physical feature. Now come on there must be some attraction to the person in some sort of way, but magnets are drawn to each other not based upon how they look on the outside, but what they possess internally.*

It is important that you connect with someone on a more internal level than just merely outward attraction. Do they make you laugh or smile or feel good or increase your confidence or help you fulfill your purpose? You want to make sure that you connect with the person internally on a spiritual level. Even after the physical attraction wears off, there will be something that causes you to stay connected to the person. Proverbs 31:30 says beauty fades and charm is deceptive.

The Need for Companionship

*G*od said it is not good for man to be alone. That is interesting because Adam was all by himself for a while. He was single carrying out the work of naming animals and tending to the garden. Which by the way, if you are single you should be working and focusing on carrying out your personal, specific assignment. God said it is not good for Adam to be alone. God made the woman for him to have companionship. I believe that women can get along without men a little bit easier than men can get along without women. Women have the ability to stay single longer than a man can.

In most cases if a man is widowed, he marries again much faster than a woman does. My grandmother passed away and my grandfather remarried sometime after to an amazing woman I now call my grandmother. Women on average live longer than men so men need women more than women need men 😊. It is interesting, for instance, that women like Coretta Scott King never remarried after Martin Luther King, Jr. was killed. Men need women. Adam needed a mate, a companion, someone comparable and compatible to him.

God placed this need in Adam to have a companion. The more

Adam named the animals and saw them two by two with their mates the more he said wait a minute something is missing in my life. He noticed there was no one for him. He said wait a minute, I need a mate. Notice none of the animals could satisfy the hunger God put in Adam's heart. I imagine as Adam is assessing the animals - their shapes, their size, and their smells - he realizes they are not compatible.

Adam did not get desperate while he had the desire; he waited for God to give him the one He designed for him to have. He did not try to make something fit that was not supposed to. He did not mate with a monkey, he did not choose a baboon as his bride, or get down with a dog; he waited for the right one. Do not settle for a dog! Do not partner with a pig! Wait until God connects you with the right one!

Some people's problem with dating is waiting. They get intimate with individuals God never intended for them. I know you have a desire, but do not settle for the first thing you see. Do not get desperate, wait and get the ideal one God designed for you. Let God prepare the person He has. God will present that person to you that He has for you. That is what God did for Adam; God worked on it. God put Adam to sleep and He handcrafted and designed a woman just for him specifically. God did not just give him the desire; He gave him the one He designed for him to have. You must know that if God gave you the desire for someone, He will give you the one He designed for you to have.

Psalm 37:4 – "Delight yourself also in the LORD, and He shall give you the desires of your heart."

Look at the process: God planned for Adam to have a wife. God prepared her. God presented her to Adam. Then God performed the wedding ceremony. This is a picture of a match made in Heaven. God had a hand in the whole process. That is what you want to make sure of if you are single and searching, and that is that God has a hand in your marriage. God brought her to Adam as a surprise. He said, "Adam I got a surprise for you. I want to introduce you to someone. Her name is Eve. She is for you."

Can you imagine how beautiful this first wedding was? It all took place on a Paradise Island with beautiful, tropical scenery. The cathedral of the sky. The canopy of beautiful trees and luscious green grass, along with bouquets of flowers that decorated the wedding aisles for miles. Every exotic creature imaginable bore witness to this spectacular spectacle of Adam and Eve experiencing Holy Matrimony.

This was truly a match made in Heaven, as God the father held Eve on His arm and presented her to Adam for the first time. Adam was speechless and he can barely say a word as he sees his new bride for the first time. He manages to utter one word he says WOE-MAN! As he pulled the veil off Eve's face to give her a kiss. I can hear the artist formerly known as Prince singing in the background could you be the most beautiful girl in the world. In fact, to him she was so beautiful he was convinced that she was the reason that God made a girl.

The Need for Compatibility

*G*od gave Adam someone comparable to him and someone compatible for him. Someone like him but different from him. Notice God gave Adam one woman. He did not give him another man. That would defeat the purpose and be out of order. It was not God's design that a man be with another man or a woman be with another woman in marriage. That is not natural and neither would it have been compatible. God told them to procreate; two partners with the same sexual parts cannot procreate.

Also notice God gave him one woman - that is God's design. Polygamy was not His purpose. In Adam's eyes Eve was the only other woman in the world and that is the way it was designed by God and that was for one woman to be with one man.

Adam says this is bone of my bone and flesh of my flesh. He is not just talking about anatomy. What he says is this is what I have been looking for. Thank you, Lord! She is so much like me; she is bone of my bone and flesh of my flesh. This is an expression of joy and excitement. Marriage is supposed to be an enjoyable thing. It was not intended to be miserable, but enjoyable. God designed marriage to meet the deepest psychological, emotional, physical and spiritual needs of a person. God's design was that marriage be enjoyable, not miserable.

Joke: A man was crying over a tombstone at a cemetery. He was just wailing and saying why did you have to die why, why, why did you have to die. A man standing close by visiting another lost relative said Sir, I am sorry. Is that your wife? The man said no it is my wife's first husband.

Marriage was not meant to be miserable, but enjoyable. Husbands and wives are to work together as allies not adversaries. Make sure you get someone compatible; make sure you get the right one. Make sure you get the right one or you may be crying for the rest of your life.

You must make sure that the person you connect with is compatible – their personality, their needs, their goals, their spiritual views, their attractiveness, all of this. Make sure it is someone whose needs you can meet and someone who can meet your needs.

Compatibility is so important because it involves making sure that you have the right fit and the right match. In fact, you may find someone who is attractive to you, but you are not compatible. I call compatibility sticking and staying power. It is the ability to stay and stick. Lady Roxie and I have two different phones. They both do the same thing, but they are different makes and models. They are both phones, but they require different chargers. I cannot use her charger because it is different and isn't compatible with the phone I have. My children all have iPhones and I can use their chargers because they are compatible.

In the same way we must make sure that we connect with someone who is compatible to us and who can charge us and meet our needs, not just our physical needs but also our psychological and emotional needs. Someone who can recharge us and help us be the absolute best we can be and someone who can help us fulfill our purpose. You need someone who fills you with joy and with confidence and assurance. God said that Eve would be Adam's help mate suitable to him.

Support is Essential

God designed Eve to be a helper to Adam. The word helper (also means fitting or fitting for him) is a noun; it is not a verb. He did not just need a buddy to help him name animals and pick fruit. The idea is someone who is going to cooperate with him. Someone who would be an asset and addition to him. Someone who would make him more than he could be without them. A partner who would help him reach his full potential - to carry out his God-given assignment.

Adam could not be nor do all God called him to be or do without Eve. He needed Eve essentially to complete him. Eve was to make up that part that was missing or lacking in Adam's life.

Notice God took a part of Adam to form Eve, so something was missing from Adam. It is not until God put her back on his side that Adam was complete and gained the part of his life that had been missing. I believe every man has a missing piece in his life and it is not until he gets the right woman by his side that he is complete.

Proverbs 18:22 says, "He who finds a wife finds a good thing, and obtains favor from the LORD."

Sis, you are a good thing. Do not let anyone tell you any different.

You do not have to chase behind anybody. Carry yourself in a way that says you really do not know what you are missing out on by not being with me.

There is a well-known film called *Jerry McGuire*. In the movie Tom Cruise and Renee Zellweger are married. She has been supporting him all the way, but he neglects her and discovers he cannot make it without her and comes in front of her friends and says I love you and I need you in my life! You complete me!

See the wife is not the other half, she is the better half. A man is only half of the person he could be until he receives the person God has for him. The Husband and Wife are to assist each other in reaching their God given goals. He is to help lift her and she is to help him fulfill his task. Please note: Adam had the task of naming animals and tending to the garden. The wife was there to support him in that, and he was to support her in her task. It is important for husbands and wives to be supportive of one another and not to compete with each other but help to complete each other. Not to hold each other back and hinder one another, but to help each other fulfill their individual God given purpose and their collective God given purpose. I do not want to downplay the role and purpose of Eve. While Adam had headship, Eve was helping him carry out the call God placed on his life. Though Eve is not always out front she is behind the scenes and her contributions were significant. Most of the time women are making moves to cover their husbands and their homes behind the scenes.

There was a western comedy that came out in 1968 starring Don Knotts called The Shakiest Gun in the West. Don Knox who was the lead actor was a naive city slicker from Philadelphia who goes west to open a dentistry. Along the way he ends up marrying a woman who happened to be a sharpshooter, but he doesn't know. Several incidents occurred where Knotts had encounters with gunmen. Each time he comes out victorious and earns a name for himself as a slick gunman. However, each time, unbeknownst to him, it is his wife who is behind the scenes shooting down his opponents and protecting him. The only way he was able to survive or succeed is each time he has his sharp shooting wife working behind the scenes helping him to look good and do good, helping him to fulfill his purpose.

There are a countless number of sharp shooting sistas who can testify that sounds like their story. They have been behind the scenes making things happen inside and outside of the home helping their man and their family succeed.

A sharp woman is supportive of her husband, helping him to stand, succeed and survive – helping him to look good and to fulfill his purpose.

Proverbs 31 speaks of the virtuous woman. She is strong and she is sensible. It says her husband is well recognized and received in the gate. The heart of her husband trusts safely in her. She shall do him good and not evil all the days of her life. Her husband is known in the gates. God gave Eve to Adam as a partner, a helpmeet suitable to support.

Sharing is Essential

A true love sent from Heaven involves sharing between two parties in order for a relationship to really work out the way it is supposed to - there must be sharing. If you are selfish, your relationship will not make it, or the other person will be miserable. A relationship involves you, but it is not all about you! A relationship should be two people working together like on a seesaw or teeter totter.

When I was a kid there was an apparatus called the seesaw. It went up and down and the way it worked was for one person to get on one side and another person get on the other side. You would use your weight and go down lifting the other person up on the other end. After they went up their weight would naturally bring them down and lift you up. It was two people coming together to support each other and share in the enjoyment of the activity together. That is the way a successful relationship works. Its two people coming together and taking turns to lift each other up.

Marriage is like a business merger, when two companies come together, they merge their manpower and resources. When you come into a new relationship it involves giving up some of your own independent rights and your own personal desires and merging with someone else. There are several examples of businesses merging successfully and then there are also examples of those businesses failing to merge properly. In each successful merger there were concessions made and there were compromises.

Some people want to be married but remain sole proprietor where they hold onto their money and their identity. These women want to remain independent of their partners. They want to act as if they are single, still come and go as they please while handling their resources separately. They make decisions without concern for how it affects their partner. They want somebody to go half on the rent, but that is it. These women want to have their partner there for other wants while they themselves live and want to be free.

I encourage couples to operate as one. Couples should refrain from using terms like my, mine and yours. Instead they should use terms like ours. These are our resources. This is our house. These are our kids. These are our collective bills. These are our cars. These are our goals. This is our debt. These are our children (if it is a blended family). Adam and Eve were to become one in every aspect of their relationship if it was to work as one.

A house must be united if it is to stand and if it is divided in anyway it will fall. When a home has cracks at its foundations the process of collapsing begins. Many homes in California in 2015 fell and collapsed. They had beautiful exteriors, but the foundations cracked and consequently the entire home fell.

Marriage is a joining of yourself to a person, your partner. That means you give up your independence. Now you must respect your partner's opinion. Consult with them before making purchases or decisions and discuss your moves with your partner.

It is a partnership not a sole proprietorship. Your partner has a say in the direction of the home, in the spending of money, in disciplining the children. If you do not want that, you really do not want a soul partner, you want to remain a sole proprietor.

1 Corinthians 7:4 says, "The wife does not have authority over her own body, but the husband does. And likewise, the husband does not have authority over his own body, but the wife does."

Now Adam and Eve were in love, but they still had to learn each other. Adam would have to bring her up to speed about the Garden of Eden, the tree of good and evil, and the names of the animals and all the things he was made responsible. The two were to become one. He would have to teach her the language they spoke, and they would develop that language and learn each other. In the same way in a relationship both individuals have the responsibility of learning each other's love language.

Now the husband has the primary responsibility of learning the wife. Men are easy to figure out. God doesn't tell wives to dwell with their husbands in understanding.

1 Peter 3:7 says, "⁷ Husbands, likewise, dwell with them with understanding, giving honor to the wife, as to the weaker vessel, and as being heirs together of the grace of life, that your prayers may not be hindered."

God hooked it up for Adam, the man, to take the lead in the partnership. He was created first. So, he had the responsibility of learning Eve. She was weaker, more fragile, and complex. She had a lot of questions. They were in love but had to learn each other. You do not just love each other; you have got to learn each other.

See when you get married that is not the end; that is the beginning. You are in love but you both still need to learn each other's personality, likes, and dislikes. Both people must become bilingual. This takes time and work and patience to really be able to learn how to effectively communicate. Understand your partner. We all come from different backgrounds, and the way love was shown and expressed was different.

The Process of Blending

When God brought Adam and Eve together it was so that they would stay together forever. I thought about when we were children, we would see names of people carved into our desk in public school and it would say something like David + Keisha = 2gether 4ever.

In fact, think about it. God made it to where Eve was the only woman for Adam! In fact, Eve was the only woman on planet Earth. There was only one woman on the planet for Adam to concentrate on and look at and give attention to. Ladies wouldn't that be wonderful if there were no other women for your man to be distracted by.

Genesis 3:24 says the two shall become one. In other words, we all come from different backgrounds. When it comes to marriage two people merge and everything starts to change. He says and so shall a man leave his mother and father and be joined to his wife.

Adam tells Eve you are bone of my bone and flesh of my flesh. So shall a man leave his mother and father. The problem in some cases is that some people have failed to cut the emotional umbilical cord of leaving parents. Realize your relationship with your partner is supreme to the one with the relationship you have with your mother, father, sister, girlfriends, etc.

When you get married no longer do your siblings, your mother, or father dictate the direction of your home or the governance of your home. No longer do those relationships take precedence but your marriage takes precedence.

The world recently watched as the Duke and Duchess of Sussex, Prince Harry and Meghan Markle, recently decided to split with the Royal family and give up their Royal titles and roles. I applaud Prince Harry because he decided to do what he felt was best for his immediate family over the wishes of the Royal family.

It is absolutely important that when you start a new relationship you focus on building that union and work at not bringing everything from your previous family and former union into the new union.

Once you are married it is important that each person works to complement their partner rather than criticizing and comparing their partner to their parent or anyone else. Do not, I repeat do not criticize and compare your spouse to your mother or father. Do not expect for things to be done in your former home nor always try to do things the way your family did them.

Joke: One man nagged his wife about her cooking, and he said, "when are you going to start making biscuits like my mother did?" She said, "when you start bringing in the kind of dough my daddy did."

See when a couple comes together, they come together and form a whole new bond. They form a whole new family unit. As a matter a fact have you ever noticed when two people have been together for a while they start looking alike and acting and talking alike. In fact, you no longer see them as individuals, but you begin to see them as a pair and refer to them as a pair – Bill and Hillary, Michelle and Barack, Jay-Z and Beyoncé.

Some people will name their children a mixture of both names. Tyrone and Shaneeka have a baby and name her Tyreeka, whether its male or female. It is like when you mix two colors blue and green, you get the color purple.

The Process of Bonding

W hen two people come together in a marriage a brand-new family is born and it instantly becomes a blended family. There is the merging of backgrounds, different ways of doing things, traditions, taste in food, in style, in clothes, ways of seeing things, and you are blending it all together.

When two people come together, they should naturally begin to blend into one. As stated before, it is like the creation of a brand-new color. When you take yellow and red, you get orange; and when you take black and white, you get gray. These colors lose their former identity and now they form a whole new color and entity. Their properties become one. Both colors lose their identity and you can never change them back. They give up their former identity; they are no longer two but become one with the one they have merged and with connected with.

Genesis 2:24 says, "Therefore a man shall leave his father and mother and be joined to his wife, and they shall become one flesh."

A man shall hold fast - cleave to his wife - in other words, he is fastened like a buckle.

The idea of cleaving is like Velcro. It snaps into place and is meant to be connected. Cleave in Genesis 2:24 deals with permanence; it means to weld or glue. When two pieces of paper have been glued together there is no way you can pull them apart, if you do it will damage both pieces of paper. God designed that marriage be permanent. It is not until we both shall love, but until we both shall live; it is not until disagreement do us part, but death do us part. Eve was always to be a permanent part of Adam. This first marriage demonstrates God's original design for marriage. It also shares with us something deeper God was seeking to demonstrate.

God uses this match that was made in Heaven between Adam and Eve to demonstrate Jesus' relationship with His Church. The Church is referred to as the Bride of Christ. One day we the church, Christ's Bride, will be presented to Him a glorious bride without spot or wrinkle. It is interesting that the Bible opens with a wedding and it closes with a wedding.

Revelation 22:17 – And the Spirit and the bride say, "Come!"

The greatest match made in Heaven is not between a man and a woman, but between God and His people. Whether you are single, married, divorced, whatever your status is, Jesus is making a proposal to you today. He is asking for your hand and heart in marriage.

There is a song by CeCe Winans that says He is coming soon. It goes on to say that while you are working and waiting, there's still room. No one knows the day nor the hour when he (the groom), shall appear, but we hold fast in knowing he is coming soon for his bride.

DEVOTIONAL AND GROUP DISCUSSION SESSION

Study Guide Notes and Observations for Singles Small Groups and Couples to Study Together

What stood out to you most in this section?

What did you discover that you had not previously known or thought about?

In what ways has this section helped you?

In what ways has this section challenged you?

What areas in this section do you agree with?

Are there any areas in this section where you disagree with the author?

LOVE & VERSES II

What a Girl Wants, What a Guy Needs

Ephesians 5:22-29 (NKJV)

²² Wives submit to your own husbands, as to the Lord. ²³ For the husband is head of the wife, as also Christ is head of the church; and He is the Savior of the body. ²⁴ Therefore, just as the church is subject to Christ, so *let* the wives *be* to their own husbands in everything.

²⁵ Husbands, love your wives, just as Christ also loved the church and gave Himself for her, ²⁶ that He might sanctify and cleanse her with the washing of water by the word, ²⁷ that He might present her to Himself a glorious church, not having spot or wrinkle or any such thing, but that she should be holy and without blemish. ²⁸ So husbands ought to love their own wives as their own bodies; he who loves his wife loves himself. ²⁹ For no one ever hated his own flesh, but nourishes and cherishes it, just as the Lord *does* the church.

*I*t is been said that men are from Mars and women are from Venus. That God has wired us uniquely different. Men and women both have different needs and wants when it comes to what they are looking for in love relationships. When two people meet and come together in a relationship both parties have wants and needs.

As I have already noted, most of the time we enter a relationship with a selfish mentality instead of a selfless mentality. We come into a relationship and our mindset is what is in it for me. How can I be fulfilled? How will being with this person benefit me?

That is cool. There is nothing wrong with seeking to be satisfied in your relationships. In fact, you should be. However, it is important we understand that when it comes to love relationships, we are not to merely look out for our own interest, but the interest of the other person as well.

Realize love is a give and take situation and sometimes in a relationship you give more than you take. Sometimes you take a lot more than what is given back to you. However, each person in the relationship has a responsibility and a role to play in working to make that relationship work.

In Ephesians 5:22-33 God outlines the roles and responsibilities both husbands and wives have to each other. God gives us guidelines as to how we can help meet each other's needs and achieve harmony in our homes. He addresses both husbands and wives; however, he spends more time addressing the husband's responsibilities to the wife more so than the wife's responsibility to her husband. God starts and says wives submit to your husband.

Paul shares with the husband and the wife the responsibilities they both have to Christ and to each other. This passage provides us with three major cords for couples. Elements they must have to make their marriage work and keep it from being torn to shreds. Let me give them to you. First there must be respect, then romance, then reverence. Let's expand on this now.

A Guy Needs Respect
as the Head

*H*e says wives submit to your husband. I just lost some ladies right there. That word to them is a turn off and it sounds abrasive and sharp. Submit means to come under. This means to align oneself under the authority of another. It is a military term. In the military they follow rank, and a hierarchal structure failure to do so leads to chaos and confusion in combat and war. So, in love and war there must be structure. Submitting is not to be done forcefully, but willingly. The husband is not to force his wife into submission.

The husband doesn't work to wrestle his wife down like a wrestler, putting her into a hold forcibly trying to make her follow him. He doesn't put her in a head lock and wrestle her into submission. It is not to be an aggressive thing, but a graceful thing. The husband doesn't roll up on his wife saying, "Put some RESPECT on my name!"

However, God has ordained the husband to be the head and for the wife to come up under him. Every home and household needs a head. God established the husband as the head over his household. He is the one with the chief responsibility and oversight of the home.

1 Corinthians 11:3 says, "But I want you to know that the head of every man is Christ, the head of woman is man, and the head of Christ is God."

Now it is important to note that just because God gives man headship doesn't mean that the woman is inferior. God designed men and women different, but different does not mean deficient. God made men stronger. Our physical structures are obviously stronger. Look at the animal kingdom. The male lion is stronger and more powerful than the female lion. Now the female lion is fiercer than the male lion and does most of the hunting for the home by the way. They are different but the female lion is not deficient.

The reason God made men and women different was so that men and women can fulfill our own unique roles. Man has a stronger physique because it is God's design that the man be the head. There is responsibility that comes with the role of being the head. In Genesis 3:17 God held Adam accountable for Eve's actions. Notice there is more said here in Ephesians 5 in regard to how the man is to treat the woman. As stated before, double is said as to what the man's responsibility is versus the woman's responsibility.

So ladies, yes, it is true that husband is designed to be the head of the home. He is the one with the chief responsibility and oversight of the home. Your man needs you to come up under him and allow him to lead. He desperately needs you to follow him and to have faith in him.

He needs you to come up under him and submit to him. Not only does he need you to submit to him, but you also need to support him. Get behind him and help make sure that you are helping the home to succeed. See ladies, the best way you can respect your husband is by letting him lead you. You must decide to build him up. Do not critique and criticize his every decision and constantly critique his moves.

Get behind his ideas. Show him that you trust him. Show him that you are his co-pilot. A co-pilot is a qualified pilot who assists or relieves the pilot, but who is not in command. A good co-pilot is there to help the pilot and crew reach their destination without crashing. You are there to make sure all systems are a go; you are there to help him navigate through turbulence. When you have his back and you are his wing man watching out for him. When a man gets a woman like that he will lead better.

The way the family has been divided, destroyed and even redefined within our culture has left our society in a great dilemma. Many men and women these days have not seen strong male leadership and in some cases a male presence in the home. For many people this is foreign to them and strange. So, we have passive men and aggressive women. Some couples come together unsure of the man or the woman's role, especially if neither grew up with a strong male to lead. This creates communication problems and issues.

In many cases, the woman takes initiative in certain areas and starts taking charge because that is all she has seen, and the man let's her lead because that is all he has seen. The man gets offended because now she is taking too much charge and acting like she is in charge and he starts feeling less than a man and feeling disrespected; but he doesn't quite know how to articulate that.

He says things like I feel like you treat me like one of the kids or you do not trust me. He feels that she talks down to him and he is mad. The woman feels bad because that was not her intention. Now she is frustrated because she wants him to lead but he will not lead. In some cases, he wants to but doesn't know how to because he hasn't been shown. This type of scenario brings friction and confusion. A man needs to feel he is respected first and foremost as head of his home.

There are plenty of ladies who are looking for a man to connect with and follow, but they need to know he knows where he is going. No one wants to follow or submit to someone who is lost and without clear direction and vision. Having said that, ladies once you see your husband is a credible leader and man to follow, it is your job to come under him and undergird him and not undermine him. It is your job to submit yourself to him and not seek to supplement him.

Men in order to get your woman to come up under you, you have got to lead her. You have got to build credibility with her. You have got to show her that you are taking the family somewhere. You cannot make dumb decisions and get mad because your wife doesn't just go along with it. Women like security. That is why they try to tell you where to go when you are driving among other things. Ladies, ya'll know I am telling the truth. Women like to know they are with a man who will get things fixed, make sure the bills get paid, and will not put the household in a bad predicament.

A Guy Needs Respect in the Home

I believe that the average woman wants a man who will lead and take charge. Most women want to follow a man who has vision and some direction. Men, and if you have vision and direction, a good woman will follow you and come under you. But you must know where you are going.

You have to begin to demonstrate you are fit to follow by making the right decisions and choices and prove that you are taking your wife and family somewhere. Say stuff like honey I know we are down right now, but we are going to get out of this. Sweetheart, one day I am going to provide a better place for you. Stick with me, girl. Work with me. I plan on having a better career. We are going to get out of debt and clear our credit. We are going to go to church and I am going to start leading us in prayer every morning and night. Stay with me, girl, I am going somewhere.

If you are not going anywhere nor talking about leading you are not doing what is necessary, that is when a woman takes charge and gets frustrated. A woman will work with you if you look like you are working on something.

Michelle Robinson was doing well and was successful. She was assigned to mentor a young man named Barack Obama who was new to the firm. She had more than him in the beginning, but she believed in him and she saw he was going somewhere. She submitted herself to his leadership and let him lead her. He led them all the way to the White House where he would successfully lead the United States as president for eight years and together they inked a 65-million-dollar book deal. Behind every successful man is a supportive woman. Matter of fact, this is for sisters, stand by your man. I know he doesn't have much now, but if he is a good man trying to do something, stand by your man.

When Lady Roxie and I got together she had finished college and was making more than me at that time. I was a struggling small business owner in college trying to get stuff off the ground. She never held over my head that she made more or that she was more educated. In fact, because she was more skilled, she helped me. She deciphered my chicken scratch and typed out my sermons early on. She helped upgrade me and gave me the respect I needed. Then she left the security of her job in corporate America to follow my vision of opening up a daycare that has been a blessing to many. She has always given me the respect, encouragement, and confidence I needed to keep striving for more.

See ladies, the best way you can respect your husband is by letting him lead you. Even if you are more educated, make more than him, even more spiritual, he is still the head. Help him by building him up and adding value to his life. The Bible says a wise woman builds her house, but a foolish woman tears it down with her hands. You have to decide to build him up. You have to tell him you are my strong brother.

Notice it says submit yourself to your husband as unto, the savior. Your attitude should be, *"Save me I want to be saved!"* That ought to be your attitude. Bring him problems and tell him you cannot fix but you need his help. Bring him a jar of peanut butter and tell him to open it for you because he is stronger. Learn to be a damsel in distress! Men like to think they helped fix problems, solved some stuff, and saved the day. If you do not make him feel that way it will be hard for him to feel respected or even needed. Let him feel as if he is your savior.

Make him feel like a superhero. Pretend he is Underdog and you are his Polly Purebred. He is Superman and you are Lois Lane. He is Spiderman and you are Mary Jane. Tell him you can always count on him to come through. He is always right on time. You do not know what you would've done had he not been there. He never lets you down. He is always there to save the day. Make him feel respected.

Get a cheerleading outfit, a mini skirt, some tennis shoes, some pom poms, a ribbon, some afro puffs, and cheer him on. Create a cheer just for him. Use different cheers when he is down and something he is working on isn't working or going his way. Cheer him up and say, *Daryl, Daryl he is our man if he cannot do it no one can!* When he is up and doing well, cheer him on and say we are the best, we cannot be beat. Tell him what a wonderful provider he is and what a hard worker he is and how you appreciate his efforts of getting things done.

Recently I sat down to watch a movie called *The Wife* starring Glenn Close. She plays the wife of a critically acclaimed author who is the recipient of the Nobel Peace Prize for his works. The only thing is that his wife is the one who is actually writing his novels; so, his body of work is really her brainchild. During dinner, while her husband is receiving the Nobel Peace Prize the King of Sweden leans over to Glenn Close and says, "I am sorry Mrs. Castleview, what is your occupation?" She looked at her husband on the stage receiving his award and looked back at the King of Sweden and said, "I am a King Maker."

In other words, he wouldn't be standing on that stage if it weren't for me. He wouldn't be walking in that space and receiving that award if it weren't for me. See a real woman knows how to help make a man into a King. She knows how to help shape and mold a man into something more than what he is. Salute to all the King Makers who use their gifts, talents, and skills to help mold their men into more than they could have become without them.

Respect Goes Both Ways

The idea of respect and honor goes both ways. In fact, before Paul tells wives to submit to their husbands in verse 22 of Ephesians 5, he says in verse 21, "submitting to one another in the fear of God." Both husbands and wives should both humbly submit to each other and respect and honor each other in order to make their relationship work. Husbands must respect their wives' feelings, their input, and their opinion.

In fact, the Bible says in 1 Peter 3:7, *"Husbands, likewise, dwell with them with understanding, giving honor to the wife, as to the weaker vessel, and as being heirs together of the grace of life, that your prayers may not be hindered."*

A man should not call his woman out of her name. A man should not criticize his wife or put her down in private or in public. He is to respect her as a person and value her input and opinions. Men do not disrespect your wife by ignoring her or being insensitive to her or not responding to her or answering her back. Do not give them the cold shoulder.

Men, you can hinder your success by not honoring and valuing the woman God gave you. Not only will you miss out on all the advice and things she has to offer, but God will actually hold you back and withhold some things from you because of how you treat her. The reason Albert could never get ahead is because of how he treated Miss Celie!!! ☺

A wise man listens to his woman and heeds her advice as he leads their home. Leading doesn't mean you do not receive input from your wife and obtain her advice. In fact, she was put there to help you lead. The wife is a helper. She is to help the man in carrying out his duties of leading his family.

Proverbs 31:10 talks about a virtuous woman – who can find her? Her worth is far above rubies. The heart of her husband safely trusts in her so he will have no lack of gain. She does him good and not evil all the days of her life. It says her children rise and call her blessed and her husband does too. He sees her value.

Listen men, respect the woman God gave you. Value her insight, her input, her intelligence, her feelings, and her intuition. Seek her involvement and input.

A Girl Wants Romance – The Passionate Kind

*S*everal times this passage says husbands love your wives. Six times the word love is used here. He also uses the word cherish. The Bible is very passionate about men being passionate toward their wives. This is not speaking merely of sexual passion but sacrificial passion. *(The week before Easter we refer to as the Passion of Christ. Christ loved the church, his bride, so much that he gave his own life for her).*

See a man should love his wife so much that he is willing to die for her. Not just physically, but also die to other things such as his ego, his ambitions, and even desires and pursuits of other things. He should be willing to give up any and everything for his wife, if necessary. The wife needs to know she comes first. Above a job, a pursuit, a business, and even ministry. It is the kind of love that involves laying down one's life.

Now this passage does deal with love in the sexual sense as well. In fact, the word he uses, cherish, literally means to warm with body heat. Ladies men need body heat. Men need relations. A relationship should not be built solely on relations, but a lack of relations will seriously impact the relationship.

It is amazing how men and women see romance differently. Men think sensually when they think of romance. Women think about tenderness and shared time. Men spend some time with you and they are thinking, *ok this is going to lead to something more than cuddling.* Their idea of romance is something that will lead to relations. Women just want to cuddle and converse.

Men, it is important that you also express your love in a nonphysical way. Women long to be shown love and affection. They desire and want attention. They want you to romance them. They like to be held and cuddled. They like for you to surprise them with a romantic evening that you planned.

That means, men, sometimes you have to get out of your comfort zone and do what they want you to do. Go to the opera. Watch a romantic comedy. Go to a restaurant you never heard of that you normally wouldn't just walk into. Women do not just want that, they need that. Women were designed to be given attention, affection, and affirmation by a man. That is why some look in the wrong place and to the wrong people.

She needs you to tell her after a few kids and a few pounds that she is still beautiful and you would do it all over again and that you are still in love with her. She needs you to whisper sweet nothings in her ear, send her flowers on her job so coworkers can see, and leave her notes and cards saying you appreciate her and give her compliments. She needs you to sweep her off her feet *(now be careful with that as you get older)*. She needs to be romanced!

Men, do little things like unexpected gestures. Be thoughtful. Express your love in non-physical ways. Show your appreciation for her. When she cooks put a tip on the table even if it is something small. Ladies, recognize his efforts and never belittle his attempts at romance. If you short him down enough times, he quits trying! Show him you love him in ways he can recognize.

Titanic is a timeless romantic drama. Jack showed Rose attention and he was willing to give his life. He died in the freezing, chilly waters in order to save her - that is passion. That is why the movie was number one, because that is the kind of love women want. That is the way they want to be loved.

Most men want relations, but they do not want romance. Romance is the stuff that leads to relations. Women want you to talk to them and give them your attention and whisper sweet nothings in their ear and show that you were thinking of them and being considerate of how they feel. They want a man with sensitivity like Ralph Tresvant said. Men you have to be romantic.

Relations do not start in the bedroom. It starts with you seeing your wife off to work, sending her a text throughout the day and drawing her a hot bath in the evening when she gets home from work. It starts in the kitchen in the morning. Then it leads to the bedroom. Men must learn how to take their time and romance their wives and realize women need more time to relax and get ready for moments of intimacy.

I'll never forget a couple, whom I met with and counseled, shared with me some of the challenges they were having. The husband was complaining how the wife did not cook and was not having sex with him as often as he desired. The wife's response was, "I am not a microwave. You cannot just touch me, put your stuff in me and warm me up and take it out. That is not how it works. You have to romance me." I laughed but I realize that is the error most men make in the relationships. Men must realize women need romance.

A Girl Wants Romance – The Protective Kind

(It Says Wash Her with the Word)

A husband is to lead his wife even in spiritual things. Every man is called to be the provider, protector, and priest of his home. The words he uses in Ephesians 5 - washing, and cleansing, and sanctifying - are words used to describe what a vinedresser does. In fact, husband and husbandman are from the same root word husband, which means house band or one who holds the house together.

A husbandman is a tiller of soil and one who engages in agriculture. The term husbandman and vinedresser are often used interchangeably. A vinedresser of course tends to fruit vine. What the husbandman and vinedresser does is that he trims away anything attached to the vine that is not right. His goal is to make sure it grows and buds and blossoms into an even more beautiful vine. He not only cuts the vine; he cleanses the vine.

The wife is like a beautiful rose vine in the hands of the husbandmen and the husband is given charge to make sure she is well taken care of, that is love. A woman in a good man's hands will look better. She will be less stressful after they have been together for a while. She will be more radiant and more confident based upon the care of her husband. Tina Turner is an example of this. She was well taken care of so much so that she gave up her American citizenship.

When a woman is well taken care of and loved by a man, she will be healthier – physically, emotionally, mentally, and spiritually. That is what most women want, security; they want a man who will take care of them, not only physically, but emotionally and spiritually. She is not just a physical being but an emotional and spiritual being. Protective love – it says take care of your wife as you would your own body. No sane man will do harm to his own body. He will not beat his body, hurt his body, break his own heart. No man would put himself through unnecessary grief.

A man is to handle his wife as a fine piece of china; a beautiful, expensive vase to handle with care, remembering that she is a fragile vessel. We were moving and there were some pieces of furniture in my house I just tossed in bags and threw on trucks; but, the very important and delicate pieces I carried personally myself. See men your wife is the most prized possession in your home. Take careful consideration of how you talk to her and handle her and allow her to deal with things.

A man is to open the door for his woman, lay down his jacket so she can walk over a puddle, use his body as a human shield, protect her from the elements, pull up her chair, lift heavy things around the house, carry out the trash, help around the house, clean, make repairs, and fold and put away the laundry.

1 Peter 3:7 says, "Husbands, likewise, dwell with them with understanding, giving honor to the wife, as to the weaker vessel, and as being heirs together of the grace of life, that your prayers may not be hindered."

How you handle your wife determines whether your prayers will be heard. That is powerful when you think about that. A man's desires and prayers being answered is tied into how he treats his wife.

The husband is a husbandman. He is the vinedresser. He is to take care of his wife and keep the weeds from overtaking her, eliminate negative growth and things that need to be pruned. Sometimes I have to tell my wife to stop being so sensitive and stop being so worried and concerned about things. I come along side of her and snip things, cut things, and prune parts of her and take things off of her. A man is to take care of his wife in a way that protects her.

They Both Need Reverence

*N*otice this is not just an outline concerning the relationship between the husband and wife, but also the relationship between the couples and Christ. Both the man and the woman are to submit themselves to Christ as joint heirs. Notice in Ephesians 5:21 it says submitting to one another in the fear of God.

It is God's design that two Christians be married and equally yoked. Two people committed to God and in submission to God have a greater chance of succeeding in marriage. It is God who will help translate the love language of your spouse. If you are sensitive to the spirit of God and submitted to God, He will help you hear your mate's love language and understand how to meet their needs.

However, you can be saved and still not fully submitted to God. A lot of the counseling I personally do for couples often comes when two people are not fully committed to God or in submission to God. People come into a marriage and want their way and not necessarily God's way. When someone will not submit to God in a marriage, there will be division.

Someone said there ought to be two funerals that take place at every wedding - where both people die to self, come alive in Christ, and enter a new union. You will have a super relationship if both parties submit themselves to God. In some cases, saved spouses have salvaged and sanctified their homes and marriages because they have been willing to submit themselves to God.

1 Corinthians 7:14 says if a wife is saved and her spouse is not, she can not only salvage her marriage but sanctify her home based upon her submitting herself to God and even her husband. You must realize sometimes in marriage it will not be 50/50. Marriage will sometimes be 80/20 or 90/10. You will have to be the one carrying majority of the load – sometimes financially, sometimes physically, sometimes emotionally, and in terms of the overall commitment to the relationship.

Marriage is not a contract, it is a covenant. A contract can be easily breeched or broken but a three-cord strand is not easily broken. A covenant is an agreement between you, your spouse, and God. God did not intend for that covenant to be broken. That is why at weddings we say what God has joined together let no man tear apart.

That is why it is important that you are equally yoked with someone else who is saved and has submitted themselves to God and His standard for marriage. If they have reverence, respect, and regard for God, it is more likely they will have reverence and respect for you. Someone who does not have reverence or regard for God is less likely to have the regard for you that they should.

See it is the reverence I have for God that restrains me from doing certain things against my wife. Respect and fear of what God might do if I do not respect her and treat her right or if I am cruel to her and I do not try to please her.

I am not going to tell you it has always been easy, but Jesus has been at the center of it all. He is the one that has held us together. We built our relationship on the rock. When the winds, the rains, the storms of adversity, sickness, lack, or frustration have hit our home, our relationship remains because it was built on the rock. It was not built on career, money, and possessions, it was built on Christ, the solid rock I stand all other ground is sinking sand. I watched three generations of marriage work and it was not always 50/50, but it was a matter of meeting needs.

When they built the San Francisco Bridge the engineers built the bridge where all the parts connected, but they all sway as much as 20 feet. In the middle of that 1.7-mile span bridge, it will sway. It is concrete and steel. It is bolted and wielded together, but there's flexibility. There's elasticity. There are two towers that go down into bedrock and all the cables and everything else are connected to those two great towers. What keeps that bridge up despite winds, despite weight being placed upon it, despite earthshaking events and earth quaking events? It is foundation and it is flexibility. This will keep your relationship standing strong and keep it from failing and falling apart despite the winds that blow and the weight that will come on it. You have to be rooted in God, that is the foundation. You have to be flexible and know how to handle things in a way without crashing and collapsing.

DEVOTIONAL AND GROUP DISCUSSION SESSION

Study Guide Notes and Observations for Singles Small Groups and Couples to Study Together

What stood out to you most in this section?

What did you discover that you had not previously known or thought about?

In what ways has this section helped you?

In what ways has this section challenged you?

What areas in this section do you agree with?

Are there any areas in this section where you disagree with the author?

LOVE & VERSES III

Teach Me How to Love

Ephesians 5:24-25 (NKJV)

²⁴ Therefore, just as the church is subject to Christ, so *let* the wives *be* to their own husbands in everything.

²⁵ Husbands, love your wives, just as Christ also loved the church and gave Himself for her,

1 Peter 3:7 (NKJV)

⁷ Husbands, likewise, dwell with *them* with understanding, giving honor to the wife, as to the weaker vessel, and as *being* heirs together of the grace of life, that your prayers may not be hindered.

*I*n 1984 the Rock group Foreigner released a song called "I Want to Know What Love Is". In this song the group's plea is to know all about love, and for it to be shown to them while they are feeling it. There was a passionate plea for the person singing to have the object of his affection and attention to teach him how to love and to know what love is all about.

That is the desire we all have. We all want to experience love at least once in our lifetime. As the saying goes, it is better to have loved and lost than to never have loved at all. It is important for me at this juncture to remind us that real love comes from God. It is God who truly teaches us how to love ourselves and love others. Since God created us and gave us the need to be loved it is important that we learn from Him exactly how to love.

In the Love & Verses One, I shared in the opening of this section we see how God shares with men and women how they are to live with one another and love one another. He shares with us principles that each person is to practice. He also shares with us some specific things regarding the responsibility men and women have to each other in their love relationship.

Again, as we saw in the previous section, the wife is to respect her husband and the husband is to give his wife the romance she needs. She is to undergird him, and he is to understand her. When I marry people, I go over their vows and I ask, "Do you vow to love, honor, and respect and to render unto your husband all the duties of a wife and do you both vow before God and these witnesses to love and cherish each other till death do you part?"

I would dare to say that most men are easy to understand. Women, however, are more complicated and each woman is uniquely different. The husband is to take the time to get to know his wife and to understand her. They are both to learn how to understand each other.

There are several major points I want to share that I believe will help you better learn how to love your partner, spouse, Bae, or Boo! First you must spend time with them.

Time is Essential – Couples Must Sacrifice Time

To really learn how to love your partner you must take the time to study them, listen to them, hear their heart, and understand what their specific needs are, and how you can meet their needs while giving them the kind of love they desire. That means you must make a sacrifice and invest time in learning how to love them and to truly get to know them. The only way you can really get to know someone is by spending time with them. Husbands and wives must take the time out to really learn each other and hear each other's hearts. It will allow you to bond and build something solid, sound, and stable.

Every building that is built is first built on a foundation. In fact, the higher you plan to go the deeper the foundation has to be and the more time it takes to lay the foundation. If you are going to build a solid, sound, sturdy relationship that will be able to withstand the winds of adversity and the challenges you encounter. You will have to take time to build a strong foundation. First, build on the foundation of Christ. Then build on that by spending time in worshipping together, in praying together, talking to each other about life and the Word, and learning how to love from God's perspective.

I talked to a man whose wife booked a cruise he did not want to go on. He said ten days with anyone is taxing and he asked me to pray for him as he spent that amount of time with his wife and her family. He did not want to get tired of them and come off a certain way and cause his wife not to have an enjoyable time. He said because he realizes it is not about him, but her having a good time. He committed to sacrificing time to do something he really did not care to do because he wanted to show his wife just how much he loved her and valued being with her. Couples must sacrifice time in order to learn how to love each other.

Men, we are selfish and sometimes we do not want to do things our wives want to do. I realized that what she wants to do is worth investing in and you have to sacrifice and give her more of your time to really learn how to love her. In fact, it is important that couples take the time out to learn and relearn their partner in order to understand how to love them throughout the various seasons of their lives.

Time is Essential – Couples Must Schedule Time

*I*t is a good idea for couples to carve out time each week that allows them to be able to spend time with one another. I realize that most busy couples do not get the opportunity to have date nights each week but one a month is good if that is possible. This time must be scheduled and placed on the calendar and taken seriously.

For the last few years Roxie and I have scheduled vacations together without our children. I enjoy these trips because it allows us to spend time together doing things that we both enjoy. It is a chance for us to recharge and to share our dreams and goals with each other all over again. We do good for about seven to ten days, then after that we both need our space and a break from each other. 😊 Yeah, we do not smother each other.

Let me say this, do not smother your lover, give them space! Some people are too needy and insecure. They look for complete fulfillment from a man or woman. See you are to enjoy one another, but do not become so dependent upon your partner that they become the air you breathe. That is why people go crazy when someone breaks up with them and leaves them because that person was their everything. Your partner isn't designed to totally complete you, but to complement you.

There has got to be a balance. You want to make sure you are spending time with your partner and you want to be with someone you can spend time with and experience things together. You have to be intentional and deliberate to spend time. You have to be intentional about dating and continuing the courtship, especially if you are busy. You have to schedule everything that is important in your relationship that you two want to accomplish together. You have to be intentional about spending time with your spouse.

It is important for couples to spend time with each other so that they can stay in tune with the way their partner is changing or maturing. You will grow apart if you do not grow together. You cannot learn how to love a person unless you spend quality time with them.

One of my favorite guy groups in the 1990's was Hi-Five. The lead singer, Tony Taylor (Rest in Peace), had a special, one of a kind-voice and they had a hit song called "Quality Time". There is a chorus line in the song where he expresses to his girlfriend how much he really wants to be with her. So much that he will ignore his pager when it goes off.

What the group was conveying in the song was that they wanted the woman they were with to know that they were giving them their undivided attention and that they had scheduled that quality time with them, and it was to be uninterrupted. It is so important for couples to have that quality time set aside and scheduled so that they can give each other their undivided attention.

Sometimes I take my wife out to dinner to slow things down and to spend time with her to show her she comes first. We open up and talk about things and she doesn't have the stress of cooking and other wifely duties.

I think the reason couples sometimes break up or divorce is because they did not spend the necessary time they should have in dating and just engaging each other. Sometimes people think they know a person, but they really haven't spent adequate time with them to really know them. It is important for us to spend time together so I can stay in tune with the way she is changing and growing. You will grow apart if you do not take the time to grow together.

Your time is your most important asset. It is the only thing you cannot get back, so make sure you are careful where you spend your time. Make sure you spend time with the people you love. Those are the things that matter most. Moments are more important than money and material things. We have been taught material and money are worth more than memories. No material fades faster than memories. I cannot learn how to love you if I do not spend time to learn you.

Talk is Essential – Learn Their Heart

Time is just one part of learning how to love your partner, talking is another important aspect. One of the ways you get to know someone is by talking to them. That goes for God as well, by the way. You have to talk with a person regularly to develop a real deep relationship with them and hear their heart and know what is in their head.

The reason people get hurt and damaged is because they do not listen to learn what a person is saying. I have sat in counseling sessions with couples and they are like, "Pastor, I just do not understand what the problem is", and in some cases I am thinking to myself, the problem is you did not listen. He was telling you he was crazy; you weren't listening. She was telling you she was still in love with her kid's father and was bitter.

Seriously though, when you get with someone you need to take time, even after you are together, to talk and continue to listen in order to learn them. I am not talking about sending texts and emojis. But I am talking about talking with a person face to face so that you can fully express yourself and also see their expressions. Part of the problem I believe with couples in our day is communication. People do not talk anymore. People do not know how to communicate, and some do not know how to hold a conversation. In the age of social media many people have lost their social skills and speaking skills.

When I was coming up you had to know how to talk to a woman. You had to have some conversation, some chitter chatter, some game, some rap, some gift of gab. The songs of the 90's were about how to approach a young lady and talk to her.

The R&B group Jodeci sang the song "Come and Talk to Me". In the opening verses JoJo, the lead singer, expresses how he really wants to meet and get to know this special lady. One of my favorite R&B singers of the 90's was Tevin Campbell and he sang a song, "Can We Talk for a Minute?". Now that is how it was when I was coming up. You had to have some conversation. You had to have confidence, conversation, and come correctly. You had to know how to step up to a lady like a salesman and perfect your sales pitch. You had to have some rap, the gift to gab, conversation, game, and chitter chatter.

Then there was LL Cool J. LL Cool J in my opinion is the true GOAT (greatest of all time) of Hip Hop. The way he expressed himself in the song "I Need Love" is timeless. He demonstrated the gift to gab in that song. I remember watching every girl in school sing and recite these verses imagining that he had written this song just for them.

He paints the picture of romance and how he has to find a girl to make his life complete. He talks about all the things he'll do for her and how he can go on telling her all the things he will do – lay down his jacket so she can walk over a puddle, give her a rose, pull out her chair before dinner, kiss her on the cheek and tell her how sweet she is. Oh girl, you are so sweet. He likens being with her to DejaVu.

See brothers, you do not just need to learn how to converse with a young lady to capture her, you have to continue to talk in order to hear her heart. You have to continue to learn what makes her tick. You need to understand what turns her on and what turns her off.

Now let's remember women are talkers. Women talk three to four times as much as men. They are like the energizer bunny. They keep going and going and going. In fact, women talk so much sometimes that men tune them out. It is not that we want to, it is that we get winded and we cannot keep talking.

Men you have to take the time to turn everything off and talk. Men we also have to learn how to listen to our wives and we have to learn them. Again, 1 Peter 3:7 says dwell with your wives with understanding. You have to listen to understand them. Men we have to learn to listen to them when they talk, and we have to hear them out.

Often times men listen to hear a problem and to fix a problem, not to hear our wives. We are like *ok what is wrong* and we want to fix it so we can move on, but sometimes they do not want us to fix it, but to listen. That means you have to hear her thoughts, her concerns, her frustrations, her fears, her aspirations and dreams, what her schedule is, and what her plan is.

Women operate off of what I call the triple A battery: Assurance, Attention, Affection. Most men think women operate off a D battery. A woman really needs the triple A and if you give her the triple A battery, she will perform at the level she was intended to.

Women get frustrated and feel we do not care about them when we do not listen to them and hear them, and when you do not hear them it hurts their feelings. Men, we must learn how to listen without looking to respond but listen to learn. When a woman is talking, listen to her she will tell you what is in her heart. Turn everything off and listen to her talk.

Talk is Essential – Listen to Their Heart

*A*s couples communicate with each other and spend time conversing with one another it is important that each person allows their partner adequate time to express themselves. Realize communication is a two-way street. A conversation is not just monologue, it is dialogue. Each person must be given the opportunity to express themselves without being cut off or interrupted or talked over. That means, ladies, you cannot do all the talking and not be willing to hear what the man is saying. Sometimes ladies already have their comeback to your response, and they have anticipated what is being said. They keep a clapback response ready. Women think like that. Make sure he can get a word in edge wise. Both parties must let the other party express themselves.

Ladies learn to share what it is you want to share at the time that is best for a man to hear you. Catch him at the start of the day. If you catch your man in the evening, he will most likely be operating on auto pilot after a long hard day and now he is just going through the motions. He is probably on decompress mode so everything around him is being ignored. It is hard for a man to hear you after a long hard day because he is spent, and he is close to shutting it down for the day. So, ladies you have to get his ear when it is early.

Now you must spend time talking not arguing or debating. Some of us are good at arguing but not talking. We are good at debating, but not listening. We have to learn how to express ourselves without getting so emotional. Reason without raising your voice. Say I feel this way when you do not talk to me and this is how I feel when you leave without telling me and here are the ways I believe we can encourage each other.

Do not be a stuffer who is hard to hear. See, stuffers make it hard for people who are married to them because stuffers shut down. They say nothing is wrong, but their mood clearly indicates everything is wrong. Remember 70% of communication is nonverbal, so if I see you are mad let's talk about it instead of just letting it mess up the mood.

Men tend to sometimes shut down. They stop talking and they get angry or non-responsive and sometimes men do not know what to do with their emotions. They do not know how to express themselves. When a man expresses himself, he runs the risk of being seen as weak and when he lets his guard down, he runs the risk of being seen as soft. Ladies, you need to let your man know he can be strong and still express his emotions and he needs to know he can express his emotions with you.

Men and women, we have to teach each other how to love one another. We have to articulate and explain what it is we like and dislike. We have to be willing to say, "This is what I like. This is how I need to be treated. This is what encourages me. This is what you can do to make me happy." Then you both need to ask each other questions. Will you teach me how to love you and be more considerate? I need to know what to do and what not to do. I want us to have a happy love life. How can I satisfy your soul? How can I make you happy? How can I build you up and not tear you down?

How can I speak to you and make you feel more confident and less insecure? How can I draw love out of you? Teach me.

When you do not communicate you lead people to draw conclusions. They will not know your heart unless they hear you. If you do not say something, they will draw their own conclusions. Some stuff is lost in translation and it causes people to make assumptions or they get mixed signals or the message wrong and there is confusion. Confusion is cleared up with proper communication. You must learn how to express yourself and what it is you want so they know how to meet your needs.

I came home one day, and my wife had some food she had picked up. Because my phone was dead or on silent, when I got home, she had brought some food that I did not like. I said, "Wow I wish you would have grabbed something else; I do not really care for this." She said, "Well, I tried to call you to get you to tell me what you wanted, but you did not answer your phone." I said, "Yeah, I apologize, thank you for thinking about me and trying to give me what you thought I wanted." I couldn't get mad at her. She went out of her way to try and meet my needs, but she couldn't read my mind.

You cannot get upset with your spouse and frustrated with them if you aren't communicating with them. Your spouse is not a psychic. They are not a mind reader. They cannot read your mind. If you do not articulate and communicate with them what you like and do not like they will not know how to satisfy you. If you do not put your order in, then they do not know what it is you want. It is your job to articulate to them and tell them what turns you on and turns you off, what you desire and what you dislike, and what you are looking for.

Touch is Essential

*W*hen you love someone, it is important to understand and know how to touch them. Hugging, caressing, holding hands, and comforting is so important. The Word says husbands handle your wives correctly. Handle them in a gentle, loving, and caring way when you speak to them and touch them. Physical touch is important. It sends certain sensors throughout the body and it activates certain feelings. Touch is so powerful that a woman touched Jesus and He felt it and it healed her.

Women for the most part are more affectionate than men. A woman wants her man to touch her, to caress her, to hold her, to squeeze her, to wrap his arm around her in a warm embrace. This makes a woman feel loved, valued, and beautiful, and it shows that a man is attracted to her. A woman wants you to embrace her so she can say like Aretha Franklin you make me feel like a natural woman.

Men, when you touch her do not always do it when you want it to go somewhere. Sometimes just touch her when she is troubled or frustrated or grieving. Hugs comfort her and assure her of your presence. Do not just touch the woman when you want something; touch her to bring comfort and assurance.

Sometimes men want to touch their wife when they want something; but touch and hold her and not want anything. Just do it because that is what she needs. Just like a plant needs water to grow, your woman needs your touch to tell her you love her. Touch her when she feels unattractive and unsure and uncertain.

Women you must realize that men like to be touched and shown affection as well. Men like to be rubbed and touched and caressed also. A man likes for a woman to cater to him and make him feel like a King. Another one of my favorite R&B groups is Destiny's Child. Destiny's Child's song "Cater to You" captures what every man wants from his woman. The group perfectly describes all the things they are willing to do to cater to their men…. asking what he wants to eat, feeding him, running his bathwater and doing all the things he desires.

These lyrics capture what most men want from their woman and that is to be catered to sometimes. So, ladies remember men like affection also.

Samson, as strong as he was, laid in Delilah's lap like a baby and wanted her to love on him and be tender toward him. Sometimes women can mistake a man's strong exterior to mean he doesn't want to be rubbed on.

Some of the most ferocious beast, lions, and alligators like to be rubbed on and touched. Lions, rhinos, and alligators can be tamed with the right touch. Ladies, you can tame a man with the right touch. Men you can change a woman with the Midas touch.

There is power in touch. It keeps your union strong and together. Ladies, do not get mad and say to your husband "do not touch me". I had one woman who had not been intimate with her husband and the relationship was withering. The fastest way to kill a relationship is to withhold affection from your partner. 1 Corinthians 7 says the husband should fulfill his marital duty to his wife, and likewise the wife to her husband. If needs are taken care of in the home, then there will not be any reason to search for needs to be met outside of the home.

Ladies you have to let your husband touch you. You cannot say no I am not feeling you right now, do not touch me. Then you get mad if he is going to touch someone else. You have to make sure that you are taking care of touching your husband. If you are touching your husband, there is a certain way you know how to take care of him. Once you learn what he likes you make sure you are the one taking care of his physical needs. There is truth to the idea that if you take care of your husband, he will not look outside to get his physical needs met. The way you learn how to love each other is spending time with each other, talking with each other, touching each other and learning to love.

If you are single right now find someone who will love you, learn you, and who will lift you. Wait for the right one. Do not rush into something just to have someone to spend time with, to talk to, and to touch. Remember when it comes to love it is better to have it right rather than to have it rushed. While you are waiting on Mr. or Mrs. Right remember Jesus wants to spend quality time with you. As you learn to love Him, He will teach you how to love yourself and how to learn others as well.

DEVOTIONAL AND GROUP DISCUSSION SESSION

Study Guide Notes and Observations for Singles Small Groups and Couples to Study Together

What stood out to you most in this section?

What did you discover that you had not previously known or thought about?

In what ways has this section helped you?

In what ways has this section challenged you?

What areas in this section do you agree with?

Are there any areas in this section where you disagree with the author?

LOVE & VERSES IV

Fire & Desire

Song of Solomon 2:8-13 (NKJV)

[8] The voice of my beloved! Behold, he comes

Leaping upon the mountains,

Skipping upon the hills.

[9] My beloved is like a gazelle or a young stag.

Behold, he stands behind our wall; He is looking

through the windows, gazing through the lattice.

[10] My beloved spoke, and said to me:

"Rise up, my love, my fair one, and come away.

[11] For lo, the winter is past, the rain is over *and* gone.

[12] The flowers appear on the earth;

The time of singing has come,

And the voice of the turtledove is heard in our land.

[13] The fig tree puts forth her green figs,

And the vines *with* the tender grapes

Give a *good* smell.

Rise up, my love, my fair one,

And come away!

ust about all of us have a desire and need to be fulfilled sexually. There is a legitimate way and an illegitimate way for our sexual desires to be fulfilled. One of the benefits of being in a marriage relationship is the fulfillment of sexual relations. Within all of us, there is a fire and desire to be fulfilled sexually. Unless you have the gift of celibacy, which is very rare but for some very real, there is a desire to be fulfilled sexually. However, there is a legitimate way and illegitimate way that our fire and sexual desires are to be fulfilled. Sex outside of marriage is illegitimate, whether it be heterosexual or homosexual. Sex within the context of marriage is legitimate.

Hebrews 13:4 says the marriage bed is honorable. All things honorable and undefiled, but whore mongers and adulterers God will judge.

God designed marriage to be the most supreme relationship for mankind, designed to meet his emotional and physical needs. The Song of Solomon gives us a description of pure passion. An example of how legitimate sexual needs are met legitimately. Here we have two individuals who are in love and their love for each other is expressed in a love song. This is a love song written by Solomon. King Solomon wrote over 1,005 songs. This is referred to as his Song of Songs, his greatest hit and most popular ballad.

Solomon himself was a polygamist, and yet it appears this was written to demonstrate the ideal relationship God intends for people to have – one of monogamy and exclusivity. This song is a pure love song, not a perverse love song. It has pure lyrics, not perverse lyrics. It promotes fidelity, not promiscuity. It is two individuals who are exclusively in love with each other and they express it. Some R&B today has more to do with lust than love.

Solomon and the Shulamite woman gave us real love music. It is an expression of romantic love between a couple who are in different stages of their relationship. Its language and imagery express a celebration of love.

In fact, this book gets very descriptive. It reads like a steamy, love novel as the couple shares intimate details concerning their love life; but again, remember they are married. This is pure passion we read here. It is literally the music of marriage. This book is also an example of how a relationship should bud and blossom into a God honoring relationship between a man and a woman. It literally takes us step by step through how an ideal relationship starts and is maintained.

With Love Comes Courting – Take Time to Seek

The way the love story of Solomon and the Shulamite woman begins is with courtship. Courtship: A period during which a couple develop a romantic relationship, especially with a view to marriage. See this is the most important part of dating. I want to emphasize this – dating should not just be done with the intention of mating but marrying. Animals mate with no strings attached, but God designed that men and women are to date with the intention of marrying not just mating.

Solomon comes calling her. In Song of Solomon verse 2:8-9 he comes skipping and running after her. He climbs mountains, crosses deserts, and climbs a tower to come look through a window to see her. He makes great sacrifices to come and see this woman and connect with her.

As I am reading this, I envision the song by After 7, "Ready or Not". In this song the lead singer promises his girl the world and more – the sun, the rain, the moon, the stars, and the mountains. He professes his undying love for her and is willing to go to the depths of the world and beyond. Nothing could stop his undying love for her.

Notice Solomon is pursuing the Shulamite woman. He is chasing after her, not the other way around. Now that is the proper order of things – for the man to pursue the woman.

Proverbs 18:22 says a man that finds a wife gets a good thing and has obtained favor from the Lord. Let him find you. I believe that the intended order of things is for the man to do the pursuing of the woman versus the woman chasing after the man. Now I do believe that a lady can make herself more noticeable but not necessarily do the pursuing. It is the woman's job to make herself more attractive in order to catch a man's attention.

There are all sorts of interesting mating rituals in the Animal Kingdom. For example, female pandas leave a scent mark in the spring during breeding season. There are other examples of females leaving scents, smells, and other signals for potential suitors. So single ladies it is okay to give some hints and subtleties to let a man know you are interested but let him do the pursuing.

Ladies, you will be surprised how far speaking or smiling can go. It is okay for you to give subtleties but you should let the man do the choosing and pursuing. However, be careful with that and know there is a difference between flirting and being friendly. You want to make sure that your motives are not mistaken! Sometimes men read into things.

Solomon comes a long way in search of the Shulamite woman. Remember she is African, and a woman of color and Solomon is Jewish, but he comes to court her. He is a King and she is poor, so he goes out of his way for this love affair. This is an interesting love affair that crosses color lines, cultural lines, and class lines.

Solomon comes to court her in Chapter 2:8-9. To court means to seek the favor. Solomon comes seeking the favor of her family. The traditional way of doing things is that a man comes, and he calls for that woman. He talks to the father and the family and they investigate and have a chance to determine his intentions and motives for showing interest in their daughter.

Every young lady needs a father figure. That is a man in your life who can help you read another man and feel out his intentions and make sure they are pure and proper. When Solomon comes to see the Shulamite woman he doesn't pull up and text her and say I am outside or hit the horn for her to come out. He comes to the door of her house and meets her family so they can get a feel of him.

I met with a young lady at our church who was excited about going on a first date with a young man. She expressed to me how she had never had a father advise her about dating. She told me they were going out to eat and she asked with all sincerity whether she should buy the food or allow the young man to pay for her meal.

I told her that she should allow the young man to pick her up and take her out to eat and that he should be happy to pay for the meal. I also explained to her that it would raise her worth in the young man's eyes if she allowed him to pursue her. I gave her the advice of a father and helped her to know her worth and value and how she should court and engage with the opposite sex.

Solomon comes to the Shulamite woman's family home and, in seeking to court her, he also is seeking her family's approval. It is ideal to get with someone who your family accepts and approves. Now sometimes that doesn't always work. So, what do you do when family members do not approve? Really make sure you listen to them and you all voice your concerns because their opinions matter. You must also look at both sides because it may not always be your potential partner who's at fault, it may be your family. Sometimes fathers can be overprotective and mothers overbearing.

With Love Comes Courting – Take Time to Study

Solomon is taking his time to study and observe his love interest. He spends time observing her and her family. Song of Solomon 2:9 says he stands behind our wall and he is looking through the windows, gazing through the lattice. He is taking time getting to know her and developing knowledge about her and her family and background. He is looking to see what goes on behind closed doors.

It is important that before you get intimate with someone you take the time to do your homework. Literally do your homework and look at their home life. See, it is through the courting process that you discover all of the facts there are to a person.

A few years ago, I went on a mission's trip in Haiti with a group of other Pastors. We had breakfast at a buffet each morning before going out to the orphanages and farms. One of the Pastors I was with decided to try one of the pastries. When he bit into the pastry, he was mortified to discover there was a fish inside. The pastry looked sweet on the outside, but it was totally different than what he expected on the inside and was definitely not something he wanted or expected.

The problem was he did not do his homework before he decided to get the pastry and taste it. We explained to him that he should have asked the locals about the dish before he decided to dig in.

That is what happens when people jump into a relationship too soon with someone without properly doing their homework. They meet somebody, like them, do not know much about them, become intimate with them, move them in, and then they find out it is not what they expected; all because they did not study the person and do their proper homework. As the adage goes fools rush in or rush through the courtship.

Take your time during the courtship. Do some research, some fact finding, and some analyzing. There should be some information gathering, some studying, and interviewing. There should be some homework.

Politicians call it vetting. They have teams that study up on potential running mates and do information gathering on who they select to be their partner because they do not want any conflicts or any surprises that might jeopardize their future and cost them an election and victory. They want a running mate who will increase their chances of winning. Someone who brings something to the table and who will help balance them out.

If you are single, that is what you need to do. Before you select a partner look at the pros and cons of selecting them as a mate. You need to take the time and find out if it is really a good fit for where you are going in terms of securing long-term success.

Do not ignore the evidence. Ask yourself what their mindset is like. Make sure that you get the answers to these questions. What is their temperament, their goals, their background, what kind of emotional scars and wounds do they have? How is conflict resolved in their family? What is their credit score? What type of criminal record or track record do they have? You need to look at everything and ask yourself, can I really live happily ever after with someone who has this kind of an attitude or someone who needs this attention. Can I really have a happy relationship with someone who's just emotionless? Can I really deal with his mother or child's mother? Can I really carry a lot of that baggage they are carrying, and it not change my personality? Is the way they discipline their children going to be a problem?

What seems small or minor now can become major later. What you are laughing at now you will be lamenting over later. What you think is cute now might drive you crazy later. Now, I cannot give you a specific timeframe for how long your courtship is to be. Each person and couple must come to that place themselves. I think your level of comfort should determine the courtship. If you feel as though the person you are with is the one, then pray on it after having received proper guidance. Consider things and move forward to the next level.

I advise against an unusually long courtship. I sit down with couples before marrying them. I always cringe when they say we want to get married, but we want to get married two to three years from now. I am thinking are you all really going to be able to keep yourselves from having sex for that amount of time.

1 Corinthians 7:9 says it is better to marry than to burn with passion.

Be realistic if you are a Christian. Do not drag out the courtship because it will be harder to control your sexual appetite and passion and keep things pure. Again, sex is not a reason to get married in and of itself. Sex surely is not something to build a relationship on and it cannot keep a relationship together. There is more to a relationship than relations.

I advise couples who are passionately in love to go to the justice of the peace and become legally married and have a nice reception later on rather than have a two to three year engagement and you all are sleeping together off and on and going back and forth and then confused as to whether or not you even want to be married. If you cannot keep your hands off each other because you are so hot, hot, hot, then seal the deal. Have a nice reception, come together, and then consummate the union.

Love is Consummated
Through Intercourse

*W*e have seen how the love between Solomon and the Shulamite woman begins to blossom in the courtship stage and then there is a shift that occurs. Solomon's language changes in Chapter 2 of the Song of Solomon in verses 10-13 and he makes a proposal and says come on my love come away with me. It is time - our love is blossoming. In other words, it is time for us to take our love to the next level! In other words, it is time for us to consummate our love. To consummate a marriage means to fulfill sexually.

We know the Shulamite woman and Solomon are married because multiple times throughout the book he refers to her as his bride. Solomon says to his bride now is the time for us to come together and consummate our love. To consummate means to come together, to complete. It literally means to complete a marriage by sexual intercourse. The idea even behind the word is that two people do not come together sexually until they have committed themselves to each other.

Sex is not what starts the deal; sex is what seals the deal. If you start off having sex in a relationship before you are married, you run the risk of ruining the relationship. Of course, there are exceptions to the rule. There are couples succeeding now that did it before saying I do, and they are doing well, but not all. Sex is a gift given by God intended to be something two married people look forward to enjoying on their wedding day. It is what makes the wedding day so special.

When I was a kid, I used to love to peek at my Christmas gifts before Christmas Day. The problem was the gift did not excite me as much when Christmas time came because I had already opened it. Certain gifts, if you open them to soon, you can spoil them. Then you do not have anything to look forward to on Christmas.

Sex was designed to be something to look forward to. It was designed to be something special. A gift designed to open on a special day. Ladies, especially, see your intimacy as a gift and your virginity as a gift that you are saving for someone special.

Notice Solomon has been looking forward to this day. He says the time has come and I have been waiting and wanting to finally become intimate with you. He says the time is right and the fruit is ripe and I am ready to enjoy this night. In essence he says now is time for me to enjoy the sweet fruit of your love. I have discovered that you can eat fruit before its ripe, but it will not be as fulfilling or enjoyable as it would be if you were to wait. That is how it is when you have sex before marriage. It will be so much more enjoyable after you have waited for the right time.

Now remember consummate does not just mean to complete, but also come together. It is not just designed for the day of the wedding, but as long as you both shall live. Not just on the honeymoon but afterwards as well. See you open the honey on the honeymoon, but you do not stop enjoying the honey after you open it.

Sex was not just given for the purpose of procreating, but also pleasure. 1 Corinthians 7:2 talks about wives rendering to their husbands what is due to them and husbands rendering to their wives what is due to them, what they owe them. Realizing our bodies do not belong to us but they belong to our spouses.

Relations are to take place routinely and regularly and that is what we see throughout this book. Couples should come together regularly. We see passion throughout this book. You will read in the next couple of Chapters of how detailed and descriptive these two are in terms of their love life. What they do to each other and with each other. Using metaphorical language, it shares the sights, smells, sounds, and sensory appeal of the man and woman. She speaks of how he lays between her breasts all night and how he whispers in her ear and embraces her. They describe their bodies as a number of things - a garden with fruit, it is pleasurable and pleasant.

Sometimes people ask what is right and wrong in marriage. Does anything go? Is it all fair game? I tell people it is cool to spice it up and liven it up. Whatever your spouse comfortably consents to, then that is kosher.

Hebrews 13:4 says the marriage bed is pure and undefiled. That means it is clean.

However, you do not want your partner to feel demeaned or degraded by what happens in the bedroom. You want your time with your partner to be something they enjoy not just something they endure. You want it to be something mutually beneficial not something partially beneficial.

God designed that sexual intercourse draw a man and a woman closer to each other not drive them apart. That it unifies and not divides a couple. Sex is a way for two people to come together and to connect and stay connected. It is a way for a couple to have an intimate, personal, exclusive connection. Mind, body, and soul. Total and complete connectivity. When you have sex with someone even for a moment you have just become one with that person.

Love is Consummated
Through Intimacy

*I*t is important for us to realize that intercourse is just one part of intimacy. Intimacy is deeper than that. Now intimacy goes beyond sexual intimacy. Intimacy comes from the Latin word *intimus* and it means inner most part. When you are intimate with a person you literally become one with them.

Intimacy is when you allow someone to see and to share the private parts of you that you keep hidden and covered from public view. It is me seeing completely inside of you and you seeing completely inside of me. Intimacy is where you share your heart and dreams, fears and tears, secrets, failures, aspirations, and things that you wouldn't share with anyone else on earth except your lover.

Intimacy is the joining of two souls. It is not just physical. It is emotional and even spiritual - the joining of two souls and spirits. Physical intimacy is void without spiritual and psychological intimacy.

Genesis 4:25 says and Adam knew his wife. To be completely known and still be loved is the supreme goal of marriage and that is true intimacy.

The reason, in some cases, some people can come together

sexually and not stay connected is because there was nothing deeper there. No glue or adhesive. One person was looking for intimacy, but only got intercourse. They had intercourse, but not intimacy. Again, intercourse is only one part of intimacy.

When you read the Song of Solomon you will discover that their intimacy is not just something sexual, it is something special. They have something special, a bond between each other. They have special names they call each other and pet names they use to refer to each other. She calls him beloved. He calls her his dove.

Real intimacy is developed over time. It is learning your mate and learning how to minister to them and meet all their needs - not just physically, but spiritually, emotionally, and psychologically. Real love making is when you make your mate feel loved, and it doesn't start in the bedroom, it leads to the bedroom. Real love making is when you compliment them and perform acts of kindness and cherish them.

Men struggle with this because they do not want to talk to their wives. Men do not want to pick up and clean around the house. Then when it is time to go to the bedroom they are ready, but the woman is not ready. She is frustrated because you haven't been listening to her and meeting her emotional and psychological needs throughout the day, but you want what you want. Men again realize that you must show your woman interest all throughout the day and that interest is what leads to the sexual intimacy you desire.

Cultivation and Management

Realize a love affair and relationship must be cultivated. Ten times the term garden or vineyard are used in the book the Song of Solomon and in a number of ways. It starts off in a literal sense, because the Shulamite is a gardener whose family works a vineyard leased out by Solomon.

The Shulamite woman works to cultivate a plot of land. We then discover that she and Solomon hook up and she states my own garden is before me and my relationship is a garden I must tend. The Shulamite woman discovers that in the same way she tills and works at her natural garden, she must also work at her relational garden. The same work she puts into tilling and turning over the ground and planting seeds and nurturing the garden, she must do with her husband.

Men and women, we have got to understand that a marriage relationship takes work and you get out of it literally what you put into it. If you do not till it, tend it, plant seeds and nurture it, keep foxes and weeds and parasites away, it will not produce the fruit you are looking for.

If a relationship is like a vineyard and is unattended, thorns and thistles will grow up. Parasites and scavengers that would eat away and erode the vineyard must be addressed. In fact, the Shulamite woman says in Song of Solomon 2:15 we must catch the little foxes. The little foxes are what spoils the vine and messes up the fruit. Little foxes would enter in vineyards and eat up the crops and the fruit and would keep the farmers from enjoying the fruit of their vineyard. The little foxes represent the things in a relationship that are neglected and not addressed or dealt with; the small stuff, spoils a fruitful marriage.

Men especially need to hear this. Men are goal oriented. They work hard at getting the woman, calling her, getting cards, texting, emailing, dating, courting, and spending, but once they reach their goal and get the woman and after the wedding, gears shift.

Now he moves from pursuing his love interest to providing for his love. He works hard to make sure the wife and kids are taken care of and then the wife feels neglected and that he doesn't love her the same. But he does. He focused on providing and the wife asks questions like, do you love me anymore and he says what do you mean do I still love you? Do not I come home? Do not you have clothes? You shouldn't be wondering whether or not I love you, I am here. That should be a sign to you that I love you.

She is like yes, you are a great provider, but where is the passion. You do not tell me you love me nor do the little things you used to nor embrace me except at bedtime. See she still needs love and affection. Men like their freedom and men lose their focus. They feel like they are working to take care of you, this shouldn't even be a conversation. But we must realize that just like a vineyard our relationships need constant cultivating.

Cultivation and Maintenance

*M*arriage like anything else must be maintained to get the most out of it. One of the ways farmers cultivate land, gardens, and fields is they till it and they turn over the soil so that the fresh soil surfaces. Then they plant fresh seeds and crops so that they can have fresh fruits and vegetables. Then the next season they do it again and each time the soil gets better. It gets better and they plant new crops. One-year potatoes and the next year watermelon.

Let me help you. If you want a richer and more fruitful marriage relationship, you have got to break up the fallow ground, work through the hard stuff, remove the rocks, etc. Not just out of your partner's life but out of your own life as well. You have got to work to remove the stuff that you have that might get in the way – attitude, anger, insecurity, selfishness, self- centeredness, the way you talk.

Then you have got to plant new seeds. That is sow back into your relationship, build your partner, encourage and compliment each other. Then you will begin to reap a harvest and enjoy a fruitful and productive marriage. But do not stop there. Each year start off fresh. Do a new thing. Go new places. Try new ways to surprise and to satisfy each other's needs and your marriage will get richer, sweeter, and become more enjoyable.

You will discover in Chapter 5 of Song of Solomon the newlyweds have their first major disagreement but work through difficulties. He comes to her seeking her embrace and he is denied so he leaves, and she frantically searches for him. By Chapter 6 they meet back up and, when they do, they begin to compliment each other again and express their desire for each other again as they did in the first Chapter of the relationship. They start back dating and they continue the courtship.

In Song of Solomon 7:10 she states I am my beloved and his desire is for me. Then in Chapter 8:6 she says love flames are flames of fire.

They reconcile and reignite the passion and fire that had gone out. She says there is between us a love that can only be described as a fire. If the fire has gone out in your relationship and the thrill or the passion is gone, all you have to do is start stirring it up, feeding it, working on it, and take the effort to poke it. Start your first works over again. I promise you the fire can be reignited.

DEVOTIONAL AND GROUP DISCUSSION SESSION

Study Guide Notes and Observations for Singles
Small Groups and Couples to Study Together

What stood out to you most in this section?

What did you discover that you had not previously known or thought about?

In what ways has this section helped you?

In what ways has this section challenged you?

What areas in this section do you agree with?

Are there any areas in this section where you disagree with the author?

LOVE & VERSES V

The Power Couple

Acts 18:2-3 (NKJV)

²And he found a certain Jew named Aquila, born in Pontus, who had recently come from Italy with his wife Priscilla (because Claudius had commanded all the Jews to depart from Rome); and he came to them. ³So, because he was of the same trade, he stayed with them and worked; for by occupation they were tentmakers.

*T*he world we live in today is obsessed with what we call power couples. A power couple is a popular or wealthy pairing that intrigues and fascinates the public in an intense or obsessive fashion. Power couples are also defined as popular or financially wealthy pairings that are widely admired in an intense or obsessive fashion and influence society's expectations of what a great love story or relationship should be. Power couples may or may not be romantic or high-profile.

When we think of a powerful couple we immediately begin to think of couples like Will and Jada Smith, President Obama and First Lady Michelle, Bill and Hillary Clinton, or Brad Pitt and Angelina Jolie, or we think of the Duke and Duchess of Cambridge, Kate Middleton and Prince William. The public seems to be absolutely fascinated by these couples who seem to have it all – money, material fame, fortune, success, influence, and love. They give us something to aspire to as it relates to a relationship and love. An ideal romance and life to be lived.

Nothing is wrong with pomp, influence, power, and wealth. Couples who have managed to stay together and build successful lives are not entirely wrong in and of themselves. I believe we should not just measure a couple's success in terms of spiritual things, but also in terms of spiritual things. Scripture presents with us its own version of a power couple. Not just one that had financial wealth, power, and influence - which by the way it appears to a degree they were successful in a natural sense - but a couple who had spiritual wealth, power, and influence.

The Apostle Paul is perhaps the most powerful and spiritual influential figure in the New Testament apart from Jesus Christ. Paul was converted to Christianity from Judaism and he immediately began to share his faith with others throughout the Roman Empire. He writes majority of the New Testament. Paul wrote 13 letters or

Epistles covering subjects such as church doctrine and policies. His writings also focused on systematic theology breaking down the various truths of the Christian faith. In addition to that Paul began to establish churches from the large groups of people God used him to convert. He was a traveling missionary who went in Gentile territories preaching and teaching.

As he traveled, he made friends and traveling companions who accompanied and assisted him in his efforts of establishing the church. One group of friends he made was a powerful and influential couple named Aquila and Priscilla. The Bible mentions them multiple times. Every time the Bible mentions them it mentions them together as a pair. It always talks about them as a team; you never hear one's name mentioned without the other.

All seven times the Bible mentions Aquila and Priscilla they are together. Sometimes naming the wife first and then the husband and sometimes vice versa. One thing is for sure and that is that they were a very powerful couple that influenced Paul and are an inspiration for us today. As we examine them there are several things I want to share and highlight about them that provides us with an example of what we should aspire to as it relates to our relationships, specifically as it relates to the marriage relationship. Let's get started.

A Power Couple is a Good Fit

*A*quila and Priscilla just seem to go together like peanut butter and jelly, like Ashford and Simpson, like beans and cornbread, like mashed potatoes and gravy, like steak and A1. This power couple had so many similarities that you can tell reading from the scriptures. Aquila and Priscilla belonged together. They were compatible; you couldn't say one's name without the other. They are such a common bond and a connectivity.

As stated before, they are mentioned in the Bible seven times. Every time they are mentioned they are mentioned together. This power couple liked to dress alike and even looked like they were related to each other. They had physical, spiritual, emotional, and mental attraction and connection.

See, you want all those things in a relationship! You want someone who is there with you and someone who you connect with well. You want connectivity and compatibility. You want your stuff to click. It should be your aim in building a relationship to click on all levels, and work to blend on all levels to become one physically, mentally, emotionally and spiritually. That is why compatibility is important.

Compatibility by definition means getting along or going well together. Phone chargers have to be compatible in order to charge your phone. Sometimes they are close and very similar, but not compatible to give you what you need or to charge what you have. There are times when I have reached for a charger that appears would work and be compatible with my phone. I then find out that looked good but it was not compatible. Certain phones are wired different and certain chargers are designed to work with certain phones to make sure the device works. When the charger is different, the phone cannot work.

I want you to understand that you have to make sure that the person you connect with is compatible in the way in which you are wired and designed. The connection needs to be made in order to get the charge you need to function at your highest level. You need to connect with someone who you share chemistry and connectivity with.

You should know the way in which you are wired. Sometimes it may appear as if you and another person can build a strong connection but then you learn you all are not compatible. Make sure you are compatible spiritually, physically, mentally, and emotionally. Do not force the fit! Listen, do not force the fit! Make sure the person you marry fits into your future. If you find out in the process of finding a partner that it just does not fit, do not force the fit if it is not for you. What God has for you is for you. Come on have you ever seen two people together and you say to yourself "Hmmm, how did those two get together?" They do not even seem like they fit together or would or could be together; it just does not seem to fit.

The classic movie *Cinderella* shows us this. The prince Cinderella had danced with the night before comes back the next day looking for her. He brought with him the slipper she had left behind in haste. He looks throughout all the kingdom to find the one who can fit that slipper for she is the one he will make his princess. Cinderella's stepsisters tried to fit into the slipper, but it did not fit. They strained and tried to force the shoe to fit but it just would not fit their feet. When Cinderella tried the slipper on it fit perfectly and that is how the prince knew she was the one. When it is the right one it will feel right and it will fit. You will not feel uncomfortable. You will not be double minded about it. There will not be an uneasiness and restlessness. You will know this is who I am supposed to be with because it fits. It feels right it and it makes sense.

People often ask how you will know if someone is your soulmate. I believe there is an inward knowing that this is the one, that there will be a natural fit. Someone asked me how I knew my wife was the woman I was supposed to marry. I told them because it fit. She gave me a charge. We connected well and we were compatible. I talked to a few young ladies who were attractive and had great potential and appeared would be compatible, but it was not a fit.

My wife had the key qualities I was looking for in a woman. There was physical attraction, she had character, and we had chemistry. She was finishing her undergraduate work as I was entering into college. The timing was right! The people around us helped to confirm that she brought me energy and helped motivate me and encourage me. There was a charge!

There must be a charge on the inside. There must be compatibility. When you talk about marriage, you are talking about a partnership first. Someone you can partner with to meet the challenges of life head on and someone you can partner with to accomplish your life's goals. It is important that you get a partner, a friend, a helper, an assistant, not an adversary. You are going to deal with enough adversity, so you do not want to get an adversary but an assistant.

In a marriage you want someone who has some similarities. Someone you can build with and someone you can create something with. Someone who adds value to what you are doing. Marriage at its core is a partnership. That is why you should size people up to see if they fit into God's plan for your life. Look to see if they add to you.

When companies hire people to work for them. They are measuring them up to see what their qualifications are and if they fit into their culture, their vision, mission and goals; if they will work well. They are looking at their work ethic, experience and education. All of these things are important. Sometimes they make a mistake in hiring people who look good on paper but who prove they are unable to perform what they promised. We can do that too as people. To prevent high turnover, they take their time in the process and interview people thoroughly to make sure it is a good fit. In the same way, you should have some things that you know you are looking for in terms of bringing someone on board. You should know what you have to offer. You should know what it is you are looking for and measure potential marriage partners based on that in order to prevent high turnover and find the right fit.

Marriage is like a major business merger. When two businesses merge, they blend their ideas and approach to build something bigger and to help sustain each other. I recently read an article on successful and failed business mergers. Some worked and some did not work. The reason some worked is because as they were getting started it appeared to be a good fit and they could build together for the future. Some did not fit because although they shared some key elements it just was not a good fit. Marriage should be approached not just in terms of feelings or from a physical standpoint, but also in terms of future. As we process selecting a potential partner, we should begin by asking questions like how does this person fit into my future? That must be a factor. When you are looking for a potential partner look long-term how does this person fit into my long-term goals and objectives. Priscilla and Aquila were a good fit.

A Power Couple is God-Fearing

We knew that Priscilla and Aquila were a good fit because they were both God-fearing, they both had the same convictions and commitment to Christ - that was an important factor. The reason their relationship is so powerful and noteworthy is because both served God and both of them were believers. They were equally yoked, so they were trying to go the same way.

2 Corinthians 6:14 says, *"Do not be unequally yoked together with unbelievers. For what fellowship has righteousness with lawlessness? And what communion has light with darkness?"*

This is an illustration regarding the prohibition of the joining together of two different kinds of livestock (Deuteronomy 22:10). God told Israel do not plow with an ox and a donkey together. The ox was a clean animal while the donkey was considered unclean. If these two animals were hitched together, they could not plow a straight furrow. Their temperaments and natural instincts and physical characteristics made it impossible.

When God says do not be unequally yoked, He is saying do not get hitched with someone who is not a Christian and who is not of the same spiritual persuasion because it will be harder for you. He says rather, if you are a Christian, it is God's will and desire that you connect with another Christian. It will not be as hard and difficult for you to stay straight and to follow God.

Now I know some people got married before either one of them were saved. In some cases, you have people who have been together but neither one of them were Christians or one or both of them became Christians later on. You have some Christians who are married to non-believers or non-Christians. I am not here to pick on your relationship, but God intended that two Christians get married so that they could complement each other and keep each other straight.

When you have two animals that are equally yoked, they can help each other go straight. These animals help push one another to go forward. See, when the beast of burdens was plowing a field, they helped to keep each other on track. They helped to keep each other straight. They have the same mindset, temperament, and the same mood so it is easier for them to work together. They help keep each other in line and keep each other straight. When you hear of animals who pull a wagon or plow you will hear them refer to a team of horses or a team of oxen. You never hear them refer to two different kinds of animals making up a team because it is important that when you have a team of two animals that they be of the same species.

You need a mate that will help keep you straight. You need to be hitched and linked to a person who will push you to pray! A partner that will push you to tithe. A partner that that will push you to read the Word. A partner that will listen to and feed your spirit things that will edify you while helping you grow in your relationship with God. This partner will also keep you on track. Your partner is not someone who will pull you in the opposite direction but someone who will keep you on track. You do not want to get with a donkey.

When and if you get connected with someone who does not believe in God and is not committed to going in the direction you are going or following God's path, this person can pull you in the opposite direction or cause you grief as you try to go straight. Or they can trip you up and it is a tug of war type of situation. Now you both are tugging and pulling and exerting energy because you are going in opposite directions. You are pulling them to go to church. You are pulling them to pray. You are pulling them to tithe. You are pulling them to read the Bible and they are tugging saying no let's do this or it does not take that and it is a tug of war.

You do not want a tug a war, you want to work together. Now it has been said that opposites attract, and I guess that happens. Opposites attract, but sometimes opposites may attract but they do not always agree. See you need someone who is in agreement and in alignment with what you are trying to do with your life and where you are going.

Political candidates running for office are very selective as to who they choose as their running mates. They will pick a partner out of their own political party who is of their persuasion, who they can partner with and win. When they choose running mates, they vet the person. They see do they fit my values and the values of my party, my ideas and concoctions, and who has a record that demonstrates it. They have the same ideas, the same views, the same values. They take the same stance. They share the same ticket. They help pull for them. When they get them, they do a thorough search through their voting records, their criminal records, their history, their involvement in other organizations, their secrets, and their affiliations. They also comb through all of this before they pick them as a partner. They are asking them how they will aid in winning the election and how they aid in getting more votes and getting elected and securing a position. They do not just choose people who they like. Yes, I must have some attraction to them personally. I must. But I also must be able to work with them and trust them. They have the attitude that I must get someone who will help me win. Once they pick them, the two become one. Obama and Biden or Romney and Ryan or Bush and Cheney.

If you are a Christian, you really want a relationship with someone who shares your spiritual views, convictions, beliefs, goals, dreams, aspirations, and ideas. Mutual partnership will give you maximum production. See, you need a partner who will not just acquiesce to your call, but who will be in agreement with your calling by helping to bring out your best. Someone who is in agreement and alignment with you, so it decreases the chances of you all having a greater divide and you all going separate ways.

Amos 3:3 says, "Can two walk together, unless they are agreed?"

It appears that Priscilla and Aquila were in agreement and alignment with each other. They both wanted the same things and they were perhaps drawn together more so due to their similarities than their differences. I still believe that people can overcome their differences if they have more in common with each other. In fact, I tell couples focus more on what you have in common than what you do not, and this will cut down on your disagreements. Couples can overcome their differences if they focus more on what they have in common. Couples must focus and concentrate on what unites them versus what divides them.

Verse

3

A Power Couple is in Sync With Each Other

Priscilla and Aquila had an ideal relationship. They were joined at the hip and they were supportive and helpful to each other. They worked together in concert. The Bible says they were tent makers by trade. They literally ran a mom and pop business. We know they were supportive of each other because they worked so well together. It was a cooperative business.

Here is a couple who worked in concert with each other. Everybody cannot work with their spouse. Some spouses need more space, but Priscilla and Aquila worked well together. Even if couples do not work together, they should work well together.

When God created Adam and Eve it was with the intention that they would work in concert with each other. They both had various responsibilities in the garden and God created Eve to be a partner and complement Adam. They were to support each other and help each other through the struggles of life. It is a partnership.

It is powerful when two people help each other and complement each other. God places a person in your life for you to complement them and for them to complement you. Complement in the sense of assisting or aiding. I tell couples even if you do not work together you should work together on your goals. You aren't supposed to compete against each other but complement each other. Do not criticize each other; compliment and encourage each other to do their best and cooperate and comply with each other. Husbands and wives are to work as a team so they both can win and be effective.

In spades a good partner can read the table and get a feel for who has what card. A good partner knows how to play their hand so that they win. Partners make a bid and say this is how many books they have and this is how many I believe collectively we can win. Then the partners play their hand. They watch the table and see how the others are playing. They also pay attention to what their opponents are playing so that they can get as many books as possible. If they see that their partner has led with hearts or has a lot of hearts and few spades, but they have spades, they are careful to help their partner get books so that they do not cut their partner and play or use cards against them. They play cards that will help complement what their partner is playing so that their partner can get all the books they can. They can achieve what they set out to bid. There is nothing worse than playing with a partner who cuts your books and doesn't watch what you played.

Sometimes couples, if they are not careful, can cut their partners out. We can become inconsiderate, selfish, and neglectful. We will fail to hear and see what our partner's expressed needs are and fail to get a feel for what they are trying to accomplish. We can cut them out of our decisions and plays and act as if we are playing by ourselves.

When you have a partner, you must consider them when you make financial decisions, career decisions, obligations, commitments, and engagements. You no longer belong to yourself. You have a partner to consider. You cannot make moves and decisions without considering and consulting your partner. This is considered cutting them out. A real partner consults with them, making plays, and makes moves that are insensitive and inconsiderate of their feelings.

Do not cut your partner out, work together as a team. It is important for you to read their hand and get a feel for what hurts them and what helps them. Do not make financial decisions or commitments without your partner. Do not make moves and choices without considering how it affects them. Make sure you understand the following: how would they feel, what they think, and how they would perceive your moves.

Do not cut your partner out with your moves, your plays, your ways or words. Do not use cutting words to criticize them. Do not cut them down in front of people. In their presence or absence, do not call them out of their name. Do not operate as an independent. Do not cut them, compliment their plays.

Get behind their dreams. Push them toward their goals. Help them go back to school. Help them to get back in shape. Help them when they lose their job and you have to cover the bills. Do not cut them and make them feel less than. You were placed in their life to compliment them, not to cut them. Compliment them with your words and say we are going to pull through this, you look good, you are smart, you are intelligent, we are a winning team.

Aquila and Priscilla had harmony in their home. They were together in harmony, cooperation, and unity. There is no indication of strife, friction, or conflict in their relationship. They honored and respected each other as the Bible teaches in Ephesians 5:33 and 1 Peter 3:7. Apparently, they knew how to lovingly work through disagreements and to overcome selfishness – a major cause of conflict.

Marriage is not a solo, it is a duet. Couples are to sing in harmony. Some of my favorite singing duos are Marvin Gaye and Tammy Terrell, BeBe and CeCe, Ashford and Simpson. Music is made up of three parts. There is melody, there is harmony, and there is rhythm.

Now with melody you sing the same song and husband and wife need to do that; but in harmony you sing different parts, but you do it in harmony. A husband and wife may sing the same song but they do not sing the same parts. With rhythm they sing it together. It is important that we sing the same song. Marriage is singing in harmony and singing together.

Priscilla and Aquila are in complete unity. The two of them prayed together, pulled together, planned together, and praised together. I believe couples should attend the same church. I believe they should worship together, pray together, and serve together. A house divided cannot stand.

I tell couples there should be no his or her bank accounts. There should be no this is his money, nor this is your money. You should work to pull your resources together; put your money together. It is more powerful because a house divided cannot stand. If you blend your money and put them together then you will come out better. Couples and families build wealth better when they blend their resources.

Here's a power play move. What if as a couple you did not max out both of you all's income but what if you saved one's income over a period of time and then lived off the other one's income. What would you be able to save if you put one income in savings and investments for ten years and you lived off the other spouse's income? I want to challenge couples who read this to work at becoming a powerful, positive force for their family and the world.

A Power Couple is Supportive of Each Other

*T*t is interesting that the five out of seven times they are mentioned in the Bible, the wife, Priscilla, is mentioned first (cf. Acts 18:18, 19, 26; Rom. 16:3; 2 Tim 4:19). Normally, the husband would be mentioned first, especially in ancient culture. Perhaps Priscilla was more gifted and outgoing than her husband, but it doesn't seem as if her husband was intimidated or threatened by this. He supported her, honored her, valued her abilities, and celebrated her giftedness.

Instead of Aquila being intimidated of his wife's gifts he was supportive of her. Now even though Priscilla may have been stronger in terms of her giftedness to teach, it appears she did not try to use that to dominate her husband. He was still the one who was the head of his household. It appears that she was sensitive to her husband's needs and role and that she gave him the respect and honor he was due as her husband.

In other words, she did not compete with her husband. She helped complement her husband and they cooperated with each other. They were sensitive to each other's strengths and weaknesses. In a marriage relationship it calls for both people to be considerate of each other and to be sensitive to each other's various needs. Both individuals are to submit themselves to God and to each other. When you have two people who submit to God they can work together in harmony and build and it will not be a matter of competition.

Some brothers if they do not know any other Bible verse, they know Ephesians 5:22, which we have already discussed extensively. Wives submit to your husbands. However, it is important we realize marriage is a relationship where both persons submit themselves to God and they submit themselves to one another. Ephesians 5:22 says wives submit to your husbands, but in verse 21 it is important to note that scripture says submit to each other. It is a mutual submission and respect. In other words, be considerate to each other. Esteem each other above yourself.

It is important when we talk about the roles of men and women, we understand that men and women are equal in terms of their value and what they provide. They are different, but that doesn't mean they are deficient. In some cases, ladies, your husband may be smarter and stronger in a certain area. Men do not get on a power trip and abuse your authority. Men, your wife may be stronger and smarter in an area than you are. Ladies, if you are stronger and smarter in a certain area and you realize it, be sensitive enough to not make your husband feel small but humbly make suggestions and let him lead.

Proverbs 14:11 says a wise woman builds her house. As a matter of fact, to all my strong sisters, if you know you are strong, you do not have to showcase your strength, use sense.

Resist the urge to always get your way or push your agenda, fight over who gets the credit, makes the final decision or who gets to feel like they won. In marriage you have to be wise and learn how to work together. Do not power play with each other and have a tug of war or wrestling match about who is in control. Do not focus on who has the final say and whose opinion matters most. Also do not focus on who is more educated and who makes more money. You need to be sensitive to each other's needs. A wise husband and wife do not push to get their way. They both submit themselves to God and say God have your way and they make mutual decisions and agreements. When this type of cooperation and consideration exists in the home it clears up any confusion.

Some people have drama in their home because both parties make power plays and try to push their way and do not consider the other person. This leads to problems. It is not about you getting your way, it is about winning! Sometimes you are the leading actor and sometimes your role is to be the best supporting actor you can be. Sometimes you aren't running the point, you are to be a good assist. This is your teammate. That means throw, let them assist, and pass to win championships.

Sometimes your role in the marriage is not to be the star but to be the support. You do not run the point. You may not be the main bread winner. You aren't the visionary. You may not be the one who gets the big opportunity in your career. You aren't the one who has a business idea. You may not be the most gifted one. Your husband is or your wife happens to be. You will not be the star player, the lead singer, nor the lead actor. You should be cool with that and make up in your mind I am going to be the best support I can. Tell yourself I am going to be the best assistant I can. The NBA still recognizes players for most assists in a game. Hollywood still gives out awards for best supporting actors, those who can help and assist others. If your spouse is doing good in an area or is strong in an area back their plays and their moves and determine to be the best assistant you can be. Be the best supporting actor you can be and the best backup singer you can be.

One of my favorite movies is *Coal Miner's Daughter*. It is the story of Mrs. Loretta Lynn, a country music singer and songwriter with multiple gold albums in a career spanning 60 years. As Loretta Lynn's career begins to take off her husband begins to get uncomfortable being in the shadow of her spotlight. Gradually, he recognizes that his role was to assist her in being the best that she could be and support her and hold down the home. I applaud her husband for recognizing, in their case, she would be the bigger star and he would be her support. It is so very critical that husbands and wives learn to support and back each other in their careers, business ventures, and power plays.

Recently two great couples from our church decided to move from Indianapolis to other cities. In both cases the wife got an incredible career opportunity to follow her dreams. Both couples have gone on to enjoy and experience great success and I am so happy for them both. I have watched God just bless them in their move. In each case the husband got behind his wife as she followed her career goals.

Their Work is Powerful

Priscilla and Aquila were tent makers by trade, but they weren't just tent makers by trade, they used their business to witness. They were engaged in workplace evangelism. Tent making was a way in which they made their money, but it was also used as a platform for ministry. They shared their faith with those who came to their facilities and whom they conducted business with. They used their services as a means to share the good news of salvation. Their career helped facilitate their calling.

Jesus told the disciples in Acts 1:8, you shall receive power (Dunamis) (Dynamite) explosive power after the Holy Ghost has fallen on you. The power of the Holy Spirit had fallen on these two individuals and empowered them to do a great work. We see them embark on an evangelism explosion. Priscilla and Aquila were two disciples who were caught up in the diaspora. Verse 2 speaks of the great scattering that occurred due to persecution against Christians in Rome during that time. They had been displaced and had to relocate but they continued to carry out the gospel.

This was powerful because you have two people who used their profession as a platform from which to preach. When we talk about a power couple, this was a powerful couple who operated in the spirit. It was not that they were just powerful in the sense of having authority over others or money or worldly influence and power, but they were powerful in that the Holy Spirit operated in and through them both individually but even more so as a team collectively.

They were both operating powerfully in their gifts and in the calling to be who God had called them to be. They both exercised spiritual authority in that they helped to train and disciple very powerful and influential spiritual leaders. No doubt they had influence in helping Paul establish the church at Corinth.

We know they were powerful because they are mentioned multiple times in the Bible. They were mentioned as having mentored Apollos and aided him in his understanding of the scripture. Acts 18:24-28 says he powerfully convinced the Jews. Apollos was one of the most powerful preachers of their day and time. He influenced people so much so that they turned the world upside down. When Paul wrote back to Corinth in 1 Corinthians 3:4 he mentioned Apollos because some were playing comparison games by comparing the preaching of Paul and Apollos.

Priscilla and Aquila mentored and discipled Apollos who was a powerful preacher who was used to lead more people to Christ. As they poured into him there was a power transfer and he became even more powerful because of this couple who helped hone and sharpen him. They were that powerful and they were used to contribute to the causes of the most powerful preachers God would use to win the hearts of the Gentiles and establish His church.

There is nothing more powerful than a couple that operates both in their own gift, call, and anointing in the spirit – two individuals who are one in spirit, mind, and body. The Bible says the two shall become one and it says you become one flesh with whom you are joined with physically. They are seen as one in the eyes of God. When you talk about two individuals operating in the spirit and in the natural together, there is a cohesive force that the devil cannot block or stop. A power couple is when two individuals both love God and are determined to serve Him while using their gifts for His work. That is a powerful couple. When two people touch and agree on something, that is a powerful connection.

Deuteronomy 32:30 says one can chase a thousand, but two can put ten thousand to flight.

A Clydesdale horse by itself can pull upwards to 2,000 pounds of weight. However, two of them paired together can pull 18,000 pounds. When they are paired together, they have nearly ten times the power. See, when you are connected with the right person and hitched to the right person there is nothing you cannot do. There is so much more two individuals who are on one accord can do. That is why you need to make sure you get hitched with someone who can help you carry the weight of the vision and what God has given you to go after.

Their strength is maximized when they work together as a team. That is how it is for a couple who is connected with Christ. There is no stopping two individuals who are joined as a couple. Their prayers are powerful. Their words are powerful. Their efforts are more powerful. Their praise is powerful. Their finances will be powerful because they are completely united as one. The prayers of two people who are committed to Christ and committed to each other and who are in agreement and alignment with God's will are very powerful. In fact, Jesus said where two or three are gathered together I am there in the midst.

Their Witness is Powerful

Priscilla and Aquila's marriage was a major ministry and they saw ministry as a major part of their marriage. They risked their lives for Paul and served the other churches of the Gentiles although they were Jewish (Romans 16:3-5). They hosted Bible studies and started new churches in their home (Romans 16:3-5; 1 Corinthians 16:19).

They assisted Paul on his second missionary journey (Acts 18:18-19) and helped to birth out the church at Corinth and Ephesus. In fact, the churches at Corinth were perhaps the two most powerful churches. Paul was single but he partnered with these two powerful people and God used them to preach and to develop the church at Corinth. I believe that when Paul penned his Epistles highlighting how couples should operate, he was thinking about what he saw with Priscilla and Aquila. Their relationship was an example he drew. They were a couple that helped to transform communities and the culture around them.

God used their union to make an impact for the kingdom. Their marriage was in fact a great ministry. See that is a power couple – when you have two people who are in God's will and carrying out

God's purpose and who understand God's plan for their partnership. Realize God has a great plan for your partnership. I believe God wants to use your relationship as an example in the earth and he wants for there to be couples who help represent the kingdom of God in the culture.

If you are married already, determine to see your marriage as a ministry. Make up in your mind for you and your partner to be a power couple who contribute to the kingdom of God. Let your marriage serve as a witness, whose prayers and words are powerful, and who can contribute to the kingdom of God. If you are married, you and your spouse should work to get on one accord. If you are not in ministry, you should get involved in the ministry. If you are not giving collectively to ministry and missions, you should give to ministry and missions – that is a powerful couple.

Bobby and Sherry Burnette are modern Missionaries who oversee a ministry of missions called Love a Child. The mission work focuses primarily on the country of Haiti. I first saw them on a television special highlighting their work in Haiti. They decided as a couple that they would move to Haiti and spend their lives there sharing the love of Jesus Christ by helping to feed and clothe the poor in Haiti. They sacrificed certain comforts so they could carry out the mission of spreading the message of Christ and helping the lives of others. That to me is absolutely powerful.

God is looking for some powerful couples who can serve together in ministry and make a difference in and around them. What would happen if there was a Christian couple on every street and in every community who helped to meet the spiritual needs of that community? What if this couple spread the love of Christ and represented Jesus by living and witnessing to their neighbors? What would happen if everyone came to their house for Bible studies and insights on the Word? I believe you would see communities change and you would see God perform the supernatural.

I do not believe every neighborhood just needs a fire station, police station, school, grocery store, gas station, and restaurants that serve them. Every community needs a power couple who makes up in their mind that they are going to stand in the gap for the community they live in. A power couple who participates with the schools their children attend. You would see power and influence. You would see people coming to you for counseling, for prayer, and for wisdom. You would see a difference being made. God said instead of trying to keep up with the Jones work to convert the Jones.

I believe God gives us partners because we have a special and specific assignment He wants us to carry out in the earth for the kingdom while we are here. The partner God gives you is so that you and your partner can make an impact in the kingdom. Look for somebody you can build with. Look for somebody you can do kingdom work with. Pray for a powerful partner, if you are single, who can help you lift and pull some things.

I have to be honest. I admire Bill and Melinda Gates. They are using their power, wealth, and influence to make a difference in the world. If some people had their money, they wouldn't be thinking about anybody else. I was in the company of a recipient of the Bill and Melinda Gates Foundation, one of the first recipients of their scholarship to the United Negro College Fund. I said, "Wow. That they have a heart to give and contribute like that is amazing." I was still thinking about it and God said you may not be able to give like they gave monetarily but you and your wife can give spiritually. You can lead someone to Christ. You can lead an in-home Bible study, you can contribute to the church, and you can give the gift that keeps on giving – Christ. He said I want you to realize I have called you all as a couple to make the difference in the lives of those who are around you.

No matter how much you build, conquer, or accomplish, the glories of this life will pass. You can have all the earthly power and fame and may even be mighty in the eyes of others, but only what you do for Christ will last.

DEVOTIONAL AND GROUP DISCUSSION SESSION

Study Guide Notes and Observations for Singles Small Groups and Couples to Study Together

What stood out to you most in this section?

What did you discover that you had not previously known or thought about?

In what ways has this section helped you?

In what ways has this section challenged you?

What areas in this section do you agree with?

Are there any areas in this section where you disagree with the author?

LOVE & VERSES VI

Rekindle the Fire

Revelation 2:4 (NKJV)

⁴ Nevertheless I have this against you that you have left your first LOVE.

As I mentioned before, a love relationship and a marriage must not only be managed, but it must be maintained. In the course of a relationship there will be highs and lows, moments of fulfillment as well as moments of frustration. In this section I want to share some insights that are helpful in maintaining a healthy and strong marriage relationship.

Most people love weddings when two people come together in harmony. Couples come together to celebrate their love and there are gifts, smiles, and well-wishers. There are fun times, cakes, celebrations, treats, family and friends. Couples have prayed and received their families' blessing and they have received counseling hopefully. I have discovered that couples do not just need pre-marital counseling before the wedding, they also need post-marital counseling.

I have mentioned before that marriage is the first institution established by God. In the first Chapter of Genesis, God brought Adam and Eve together in marriage and we see the first wedding. In the last book of the Bible, Revelation, God reveals the concept of Him being married to His church and we witness the last wedding. In Ephesians 5:25-27 the church is referred to as the bride of Christ. The church is being made ready for Christ's return when He will finally wed the church and there will also be a formal reception.

The Bible says that the church must first be made ready and it says that judgement first began in the house of the Lord. It says that God is coming back for a church without spot or wrinkle. In the opening of the book of Revelation God speaks to the church at Ephesus. He says you all somehow have become distracted and you have left your first love which is Christ. The church left its first love and needed to do its first works over.

I think the very thing Jesus accuses of happening at the Church at Ephesus is the same thing that can happen with a relationship. If not tended to properly the love in a marriage relationship can go cold and the thrill and excitement that once existed can die down. It doesn't happen all of a sudden or intentionally. It happens gradually due to neglect.

I have a cell phone just like everyone else. I am bad about downloading the updates on my phone. Because I do not download the updates in a timely manner I am constantly dealing with my phone running slow or things not working the way that they should. The times I deal with issues with my phone I realize it is due to me not having made the proper updates. I am operating off the old set up failing to realize that I need to update and make sure my phone is working properly with the updates required for that season.

In the same way, relationships require updates. It is important to get the updates so that the relationship continues to function properly. It is important for couples to make sure they are recognizing the changes in their spouse at various seasons so they can make the right adjustments and updates. We must also learn how to salvage our relationships. Anytime you take two imperfect people, you will not have a perfect situation. Two imperfect people are prone to make mistakes. There will be break ups, moments of pain, disappointment, and discouragement.

There will be times you say wow did I make the right decision; did I do the right thing. You will ask yourself the question, "Why did I get married?" You will go from saying I got a great deal to this is not ideal. You will think you got a raw deal and that you want a new deal. No, marriage is a done deal! I do not care how long you have been together before getting married, how much counseling you have had nor how spiritual the two of you are. There will be some lover's quarrels, some disagreements, some touchy moments, and some issues that arise. Even if you pray, your marriage will be tested and tried. There may even be times the relationship is ruptured.

In this section, I want to help you to learn how to work through those difficult moments and help you to make your love last forever.

Avoid Relationship Rupture – Through Proper Consideration

A rupture describes when something is torn or broken or fragmented. Another definition of a rupture is when there is a breach of harmonious, friendly, or peaceful relations. In a relationship there are a number of reasons why things can become torn, broken, ruptured, or damaged.

When two people meet and come together in a relationship both parties have wants and needs. Most of the time we enter a relationship with a selfish mentality instead of a selfless mentality. That is to say we come into a relationship and our mindset is WIIIFM - what is in it for me. How can I be fulfilled? How will being with this person benefit me?

We have our wants and desires and it clouds our judgements. You have two people trying to get their way and neither party submitting or yielding or willing to negotiate and make compromises. Marriage is not just about you getting your needs met, it is about you meeting needs and trusting your spouse will meet yours. Marriage doesn't involve being selfish, but selfless. You are giving up your rights. You no longer belong to yourself.

1 Corinthians 7:4 says your body doesn't belong to you. You have to share your body, your bills, your burdens, and your blessings.

There is nothing wrong with seeking to be satisfied in your relationships. In fact, you should be. However, it is important we understand that when it comes to love relationships we are not to merely look out for our own interest but the interest of the other person as well. Realize love is a give and take situation and sometimes in a relationship you give more than you take. Sometimes you take a lot more than is given back to you. However, each person in the relationship has a responsibility and a role to play in helping to make that relationship work. This involves being thoughtful and considerate of the other person.

Building a healthy relationship involves becoming selfless. Some people enter into a relationship and they want certain benefits from being in a relationship – companionship and company. They are selfish and they are only thinking about what they get out of it. Selfishness is the mood of our day. Many people are selfish and self-centered. We are the generation of the selfies. We take pictures of ourselves, some people multiple times throughout the day. We teach love yourself first. You got to love you, and this can create a sense of selfishness.

To build a relationship you cannot be selfish. You have to be selfless and you have to sacrifice. You have to think about the other person. You have to trust that they will think about you. It involves a certain amount of risk to have a real relationship. I have to risk and trust you with my heart. I have to trust that if I give myself away to you that you will not use me. I cannot think about just me anymore, now I have to think about us.

A lot of marriages get eaten by the me monster.... me, me, me, my way, my wishes, my way, my whims, my birthday, my car, my money, my house, my career, my desires, and that destroys a relationship. It is not what your feelings are, what your desires are, what your goals are, your will, but God's will or Word.

As I have stated before, there should be a funeral at every wedding. Your will, wishes, whims and wants die for the good of the overall union. It is a sacrifice and it involves selflessness. It is no longer about me but us. Now it is what are their needs. What are their desires? THE TWO SHALL BECOME ONE. When I perform a wedding, I say to both the husband and the wife the scriptures say submit yourself to the other, yielding yourself to one another.

Philippians 2:3-4 says, "Let nothing be done through selfish ambition or conceit, but in lowliness of mind let each esteem others better than himself. Let each of you look out not only for his own interests, but also for the interests of others."

That includes your spouse. Marriage was designed for two people to work together in unity. God did not design that we work against each other, but alongside each other. God did not intend that we war with each other but work with each other and that there be cooperation with each other and consideration for each other. Husbands be considerate of your wife and wives be considerate of your husband.

Be considerate of how much hot water you use up in the shower. Be considerate and let the seat down after you use the restroom. Be considerate of purchases you make, especially since that is a divider. You must be considerate of how you spend your time and who you spend your time with. Be considerate of how they feel about your plans. Be considerate of how you have company over and when you have loud music. Be considerate of each other's work hours.

Avoid Relationship Rupture – Through Proper Communication

When you get married there is a language barrier that you must overcome. Often times relationships are ruptured because things got lost in translation. One person doesn't know how to properly express themselves and they have a hard time understanding how to decipher what their partner wants so it creates a rift in the relationship. You think they want material and they want time. You think they want your work and service, but they want love, affection, touch, and verbal words of affirmation.

When entering into a relationship it is important that you know what your own needs are and how you expect for someone to meet those needs. You must learn how to properly articulate to a person how you need to be loved, what turns you on and turns you off, and what speaks to your heart. You need to communicate this to your partner. If you are single right now, then you need to know what does it require to love someone like you? What kind of patience does it take? What kind of sacrifices must a person make?

You may be a needy person, or the person needs to know early on that you are high maintenance and gifts speak to you. Or they may need to know you are a clingy person, so they need to spend time with you. Or that you need somebody who will cook for you and serve you like your mom or a man to fix things and repair things around the house.

You may get with someone who cannot quite love you at the level you need. You may require a liter of love, but you are with a person who can only produce a pint. See, some of us love hard. We are affectionate people that is why when people betray us or are disloyal or do not follow through it really messes us up. I'll give you the shirt off my back. I expect you to do the same. I'll defend you, so I expect you to do the same.

Some of us need some Rosetta Stone as it relates to our relationships. We need to learn a new language. Sometimes there is a breakdown in communication or failure and things get lost in translation. Sometimes we are trying to be heard and felt and understood but we do not do it for the other person.

One of the hardest things in the world to do is learn a new language. Words are pronounced differently. It is very difficult to understand and to express yourself with the person who has a whole other dialect. When I was a freshman in high school, I took Spanish but I failed. I did not listen. I did not study. I did not pay attention. I did not learn the language enough to engage with someone who spoke Spanish. The reason I failed is because I did not study and I did not listen.

The best way to learn and understand how to communicate with your partner is by listening to them, studying them, and paying attention. You have to learn their body language, their facial expressions, their response and reaction to things, and the tone in which they speak.

Some of our communication involves expressing ourselves and getting our point across, but we are hard of hearing when it comes to listening to the other person and we do not listen to the other person. Be slow to speak and swift to hear. Listen to their complaints. Listen to their concerns. Listen to their desires. Understand the things they like and do not like. Listen to them. If you listen to your partner you will learn how to love them; it will clear up a lot of confusion.

If you listen, you will know that her favorite color is pink because her sister died of breast cancer and it reminds her of her sister she lost. Or she has an issue with you being gone because someone else left her and did not come back. Or that it is important for you to not just treat her lovingly but to say I love you because her father did not, or his mother never did. You would know it means a lot to him for you to compliment him because he was constantly criticized. It means a lot for you to physically touch him and hug him in a gentle way because that is how his mother showed her affection to him. Or she needs you to touch her, hold her, and caress her because she was always touched the wrong way or abused. It means a lot to buy her nice things because she always wanted someone to buy her nice things because her family couldn't afford it for her birthday or Christmas. Or she always had to pay her own way. Or he likes peace and quiet time because there was always drama, anger, and chaos in the house they lived in.

When it comes to building solid and strong relationships, we must develop the discipline of listening to our partner, not just so that we can respond but so that we can understand. Communication is key to keeping a healthy relationship and preventing a rupture.

Reconcile by Confronting the Issue

God's desire is that couples resolve conflicts that arise by confronting issues. One of the things we learn in marriage is how to confront ourselves and confront issues we face. Marriage was designed to mature you. Most people get married when they are young adults, while they are young and still a little immature. The first quarter of our lives we grow and reach a certain stage. The last three quarters we spend with someone else and it is God's design the two individuals grow together.

Marriage is the idea of two individuals becoming one. Two individuals who grow and are supposed to go through the struggles of life together. They start looking alike. They start thinking alike. They start finishing each other's sentences. They start reading each other's thoughts and body language from afar off. It is designed that they blend together, not break apart. God intends that we grow through what we go through as married people. God doesn't intend for us to melt down when we go through something in our marriages but that we mature as individuals.

We grow by praying more about the problems. We grow in

patience as we have to deal with another person's ways, wants, and personality. We grow psychologically, gain new ideas, and different ways of seeing things. We grow to be less selfish as we have children and a family. So, when things go down in the marriage see it as a chance for you to mature.

Part of maturing is getting along well with others and learning to bend and compromise. That means the first step is that you must learn how to forgive and be reconciled. Ephesians 4 says be angry but do not sin. Do not let the sun go down on your wrath. Your spouse will do things that make you mad and make you angry and upset you. You have a right to be angry. But after you have had time to vent and rant and rave be reconciled before bed. Do not let a divide build because it will increase the distance. Couples must come together and address conflict before it widens or deepens their divide.

Distance develops when there are unresolved issues and couples develop what I call a "roommate relationship". They live together and pay bills, but they aren't happy. They barely see each other, barely talk. They just live together. Conflicts are not resolved. They have a blow up and argument and this snowballs into something bigger.

To have a healthy relationship and to prevent greater ruptures and divides within the relationship couples must be willing to confront issues. You cannot correct what you will not confront. I am a firm believer in bringing to someone's wrong to their attention. Sometimes people do not know they hurt or offended you. When you fall out you have to express yourself and say this is what upset me, and this is how it made me feel. Help them to see how what was said and done hurt you.

Fight Fair. Here are some dos and do nots, mainly do nots.

- Do not use words like you always do this or you never do this. Do not criticize. Your intention is to correct the issue by confronting the issue, not making matters worse. Some people are unreasonable and refuse to look at themselves.

- Do not shut down. Do not ignore the issue. Do not check out. Do not be closed minded. Do not be a person who doesn't accept responsibility. Do not tune out your spouse; hear their heart. Confrontation must be done at the right time, with the right pitch, in the right tone, in private and not in public.

- Do not stuff things and allow animosity and anger and resentment to build up inside and you are sitting and just smoldering like a ticking time bomb or a volcano. Have examples of what you refer to that bothers you or things you have noticed.

- Do not go to bed angry. It creates greater distance and it leads to two people living together but separate. People live separate lives long before they separate. He says do not give space to the devil.

The devil wants to do to your relationship what he did to Adam and Eve. He brought enmity between them. Now they were married, but not happily ever after. Adam couldn't divorce Eve and get remarried because she was the only woman on earth. But the devil brought enmity between Adam and Eve. He wants to do the same thing in your marriage. He wants to bring division and ultimately disruption. Do not let him divide and get in your marriage.

Reconcile by Compromising on Issues

*T*n marriage you must learn the art of compromise. You will not always get your way. That is life in general. Life is not about always getting your way. It is about learning to adjust and to adapt so that you can be fruitful and effective. It is the same with marriage.

Quote: *Marriage is when you agree to spend the rest of your life sleeping in a room that is too warm, beside someone who's sleeping in a room that is too cold.*

Sometimes you will have to be the bigger person and humble yourself and swallow your pride and say I am sorry if you are offended or if I offended you, even if you are not the party that was wrong. It is okay to give a little. It is okay to meet the other person on their terms. It is okay to be right and be quiet. Ladies, especially you, you do not have to have the last word. You do not have to get the last lick. Do not live your life trying to get your lick back. Let it go sometimes. If you let it go sometimes you will give him a chance to listen to what you said, but he cannot listen when it becomes a lick contest.

It is not about who is right, but what is right. Okay, I was right in principle but not approach. Some people would rather win the argument and lose the relationship. I'd rather win the relationship and lose the argument.

Marriage laws work like traffic laws. Do you want to be right or do you want to wreck? Sometimes you may have the right of way but someone speeds through a light or violates and makes a wrong turn or move. You have to have sense enough to say look at them. You cannot push your way. Sometimes you have to do what is right to keep from wrecking your stuff and having a mess on your hands. You have to be a mature and defensive driver.

The Bible says, as much as it depends on you live in peace with all men. (Romans 12:18)

God does not hold you responsible for the other person's response but for your part. If they receive your attempts to reconcile or reject your attempts, you did your part. The next step is to pray and place it in God's hand. Some situations require God's involvement. Some things that have been broken only He can put back together.

1 Peter 2:20-23 says place things in God's hands for Him to judge justly.

God intends for couples to compromise, and when there is a rift in the relationship, for us to work to be reconciled. It is easier these days for people to get out of marriage than it is other commitments they made – phone contracts, bad debt, car loans.

People separate over irreconcilable differences, but I believe some things we call irreconcilable are reconcilable. The biblical justifications for divorce are abuse, abandonment and adultery. Even in those cases you have to ask case by case is this God's will for this marriage to end. If you can avoid it, do not divorce and be determined to go the distance. Take out all the exit signs and off ramp signs and go the distance.

Thank God that He is not like us and God teaches us how to do marriage. The Bible says God is married to us. We are His bride. In our marriage relationship there is a lot of forgiveness that takes place. We abuse God, abandon God, and commit adultery against God but His anger is but for a moment. His mercies are for a lifetime. God stays committed to us and forgives us.

Jeremiah 3:1-14 says, I am married to the backslider. He says no matter what you have done I am still married to you and committed to you.

It is so comforting to know that God loves us after we have fallen short and after we have made a mistake. He doesn't continue to bring up our faults and flaws. He continues to love us and that is what we must determine to do in our relationships.

1 Peter 4:8 says, "And above all things have fervent love for one another, for love will cover a multitude of sins."

If you are going to keep a peaceful and healthy home, you cannot carry stuff around that the other person did. You have got to cover it up and cover it up fast. I am not talking about cover your stuff and the dirt you do. I am talking about covering the sins and mistakes of your partner.

Every house has trash that you collect, but do not allow trash to collect. Discard it, cover it, and get rid of it. When it is trash in the house, it doesn't matter whose it is, you do not want the house stinking so you cover it and take it out.

Do not Let the Fire Die

esus tells the church, His bride, in the book of Revelation, that they need to do the first works over again. They need to go back to their first love. That their jobs, their careers, their possessions, other pursuits, other people and things has taken His place. See as Christians, if we are not careful, we can lose our first love for God and get caught concentrating on other things and begin to crowd out Christ.

The same thing can happen in our relationships. The thrill is gone. We are saved but we lost our spark and our fire is faint. It is not as strong. In fact, He said the fire was about to go out. He says they need to go back and rekindle the fire. Fires can easily go faint and die out if they do not have the right stuff to keep them going! A fire must be attended to. There are a lot of forces that can kill the fire. Wind, rain, cold things can dampen it. Love is the same way. People talk about falling in and out of love.

Sometimes it is like a fire that has been unattended. People grow apart because the intimacy, the time spent, the relationship stops being the priority, especially when you throw children, school, work, and trying to survive in the mix. The relationship takes a back seat and the fire begins to die down. The time spent laughing, talking, praying, enjoying each other's presence begins to die down. Do not let the flame of your fire die or fade; you have to do the first works over.

Put your spouse first again. You have to make your number one aim connecting with your spouse and spending the time to reinvest back into your love relationship. Do not take them for granted and neglect the fire and leave it unattended because the fire can die out and the love can wax cold if you are not careful.

Schedule regular dates and time together, vacations without the kids, and excursions without the kids where you all work on your relationship and you rekindle it. Do it for the kids because you cannot have a good home for them with your spouse second. It is in the kids' interest that you all have a solid relationship. They need to know your spouse is your first love. To rebuild you must rekindle and start your first works over. You have to reinvest back into your marriage. Start dating again. Go back to spending time to share your dreams, goals, and desires. Continue the courtship.

Do the First Works Over

ring the romance back and the focus back on your marriage. Plan short excursions and get away to try new restaurants. Bring back love letters, love texts and emojis, romantic evenings, or even go to a hotel and have someone else watch the children. Valentine's Day is good but you need to make it your aim to have Valentine's every week. You have got to re-invest in your relationship. You need to find a way to keep the fire going and to fuel the fire.

The things you did to capture them, you must continue to do to keep them. That means, ladies, you cannot go to bed with a head full of rollers every night. Fellas you cannot stop giving her attention and wining and dining her and keeping yourself up and being romantic and holding conversations. You have to continue to do that.

Do not take each other for granted. Just like you prayed for them, continue to pray for them and your relationship. Couples, if you are not careful you will become roommates who do not have a lot in common other than rent and other responsibilities. A relationship is more than rent and responsibilities. There has to be some romance and some intimacy where you are into the me you see.

Sometimes the fire goes out or the thrill is gone. Then you need to rekindle the fire and the spark. When I was a kid, I played a lot of video games. Sometimes I would be losing and not doing as well as I wished. I was still interested in the game and so I would hit the reset button. Even though I had to start from the beginning this time, I was more careful and determined to do a better job.

You may have been married before. You may have run into some problems with the marriage you are in. The good news is you can hit the reset button and start all over again and do even better than before and still be a winner. Marriage should be approached with a new perspective if you are going to start over again. You have to prove yourself again, make sacrifices again, and put forth some effort again to get to where you are trying to go.

You may not have all of the fireworks in a relationship you had before. Fourth of July only comes once a year. That is why you have to deliberately buy new ones, take time out and light them, and spark them up. Scripture opens with a wedding and it closes with a wedding. God officiates the first wedding and marriage and he is involved in the last wedding.

Revelation 19:7-9 says, "Let us be glad and rejoice and give Him glory, for the marriage of the Lamb has come, and His wife has made herself ready. And to her it was granted to be arrayed in fine linen, clean and bright, for the fine linen is the righteous acts of the saints. Then he said to me, write: 'Blessed are those who are called to the marriage supper of the Lamb!' And he said to me, these are the true sayings of God."

DEVOTIONAL AND GROUP DISCUSSION SESSION

Study Guide Notes and Observations for Singles Small Groups and Couples to Study Together

What stood out to you most in this section?

What did you discover that you had not previously known or thought about?

In what ways has this section helped you?

In what ways has this section challenged you?

What areas in this section do you agree with?

Are there any areas in this section where you disagree with the author?

Conclusion

As we have examined the various verses presented in this book what we discover is that the scriptures give us higher things to aspire to as it relates to our relationships. The concept of LOVE. It is my hope that after having taken the time to read this book you have been challenged to love at an even higher level. Whether you are single or married or on the relationship rebound I challenge you to love at the level God has called for you to love. 1 Corinthians 13:4-10 gives us a biblical definition of love. It says *"Love suffers long and is kind; love does not envy; love does not parade itself, is not puffed up; does not behave rudely, does not seek its own, is not provoked, thinks no evil; does not rejoice in iniquity, but rejoices in the truth; bears all things, believes all things, hopes all things, endures all things. Love never fails. But whether there are prophecies, they will fail; whether there are tongues, they will cease; whether there is knowledge, it will vanish away. For we know in part and we prophesy in part. But when that which is perfect has come, then that which is in part will be done away."*

See...the Bible gives us higher things to aspire to as it relates to our lives and our relationships, especially by way of our commitments and our marriages. It points us to a higher standard.

CPSIA information can be obtained
at www.ICGtesting.com
Printed in the USA
BVHW031654200420
577978BV00001B/18